Praise for *Life of the Beloved*

"Gentle and searching. This Crossroad book is a spiritual primer for anyone seeking God." — *The Other Side*

"Nouwen's prose is refreshingly straightforward and jargon-free.... For those unfamiliar with his work, this volume is a wonderful place to begin. For others who have benefited from Nouwen's insights, *Life of the Beloved* will be welcomed as yet another significant achievement."
— *Circuit Rider*

"A beautiful and sensitive book that reaches out to the believer." — *Church and Synagogue Library Association*

"Brings affirmation and renewal to the reader. Anyone who is searching for the Spirit of God in the world today will benefit from reading it." — *Horizons*

"Nouwen writes with a disarming simplicity and honesty. He shows a vulnerability that bonds him with the reader from the beginning." — *The Catholic World*

"Profound." — *Christian Living*

"An engaging, highly practical book about the spiritual life. Powerful." — *Whisperings*

Life of
the Beloved

HENRI J.M. NOUWEN

Life of the Beloved

Spiritual Living in a Secular World

TENTH ANNIVERSARY EDITION

WITH NEW GUIDE
FOR REFLECTION

A Crossroad Book
The Crossroad Publishing Company
New York

The Crossroad Publishing Company
www.CrossroadPublishing.com

Printed in the United States of America

Library of Congress Cataloging-in-Publication Data

Nouwen, Henri J. M.
    Life of the beloved / Henri J. M. Nouwen.
        p.   cm.
    ISBN 0-8245-1184-0; ISBN: 0-8245-1986-8 (pbk.)
    1. Spiritual life – Catholic Church.   2. Nouwen, Henri J. M.
I. Title.
BX2350.2.N672   1992
248.4'82 – dc20   92-14854

9 10 11 12 13 14 15   12 11 10 09

To Connie Ellis
in gratitude

Contents

Acknowledgments

This book was written and made ready for publication with the support of many friends. I first of all want to thank Connie Ellis for her secretarial assistance and for the many ways in which she encouraged me to keep writing during busy times. I dedicate *Life of the Beloved* to her in deep gratitude for her faithful friendship and generous support. I am also grateful to Conrad Wieczorek for the many ways in which he offered his editorial assistance to Connie and myself in the final stages of the manuscript.

A special word of thanks goes to Patricia Beall, Diana Chambers, Gordon Cosby, Bart Gavigan, Steve Jenkinson, Sue Mosteller, Dolly Reisman, Susan Zimmerman, and my editor at Crossroad, Bob Heller, for their many encouraging words and concrete suggestions to bring this text to completion.

Finally I want to express my thanks to Peggy McDonnell, her family and friends, for their friendship and their generous financial support and to the Franciscan Community in Freiburg, Germany, who offered me a safe and prayerful place to write.

A Friendship Begins

This book is the fruit of a longstanding friendship, and you will read it with more profit, I believe, if I begin by telling you the story of this friendship. A little more than ten years ago, while I was teaching at Yale Divinity School, a young man arrived in my office to interview me for the Connecticut section of the Sunday edition of the *New York Times*. He introduced himself as Fred Bratman. As we sat down to talk, I quickly found myself taken hold of by a mixture of irritation and fascination. I was irritated because it was clear that this journalist was not terribly interested in doing what he was doing. Someone had suggested to him that I might be a good subject for a profile. He had followed up on the suggestion, but I couldn't detect any great eagerness to know me or any ardent desire to write about me. It was a journalist's job that had to be done, but could easily be done without. Nevertheless, there was also an element of fascination because I sensed, behind the mask of indifference, a spirit fully alive — eager to learn and to create. I somehow knew that I was face to face with a man full of great personal gifts, anxiously searching for a way to use them.

After a half-hour of questions that seemed of little interest to either of us, it became obvious that the interview had come to an end. An article would be written; a few people might read it, and there would be little, if any, outcome. The two of us knew this, and we both sensed that we could have put our time to better use.

Just as Fred was about to put his notebook back into his briefcase and say his customary "Thank you," I looked at him squarely and said, "Tell me, do you like your job?" Quite to my surprise, he replied, without much thought, "No, not really, but it's a job." Somewhat naively I responded, "If you don't like it, why do you do it?" "For the money, of course," he said, and then, without further questioning from me, added, "Although I really love to write, doing these little newspaper profiles frustrates me because the limitations of length and form prevent me from doing justice to my subject. How, for example, can I say something in depth about you and your ideas when I can only use 750 words to express it? ... but what choice do I have? ... You have to make a living. I should be happy to have at least this to do!" In his voice I heard both anger and resignation.

Suddenly it hit me that Fred was close to surrendering his dreams. He looked to me like a prisoner locked behind the bars of a society forcing him to work at something in which he didn't believe. Looking at him, I experienced a deep sympathy — more than that I dare say — a deep love for this man. Beneath the sarcasm and the cynicism I sensed a beautiful heart, a heart that wanted to give, to create, to live a fruitful life. His sharp mind, his openness about himself and the simple trust he put in me made me feel that our meeting could not just be something accidental. What was happening between us seemed to me quite similar to what happened when Jesus looked steadily at the rich young man and "was filled with love for him" (Mark 10:21).

13

Quite spontaneously I felt a strong desire rise up in me to liberate him from his imprisonment and to help him to discover how to fulfill his own deepest desires.

"What do you really want?" I asked.

"I want to write a novel...but I'll never be able to do it."

"Is this something you really want?" I asked. He looked at me with surprise on his face and said with a smile, "Yes,

---

You are free to do what you want — if, that is, you really want it!

---

it is,...but I'm also afraid because I've never written a novel, and maybe I don't have what it takes to be a novelist." "How will you find out?" I asked. "Well, I probably won't ever be able to find out. You need time, money and, most of all, talent, and I don't have any."

By now I had become angry at him, at society, and, to some degree, at myself for letting things just be as they are. I felt a strong urge to break down all these walls of fear, convention, social expectations and self-deprecation, and I blurted out, "Why don't you quit your job and write your novel?" "I can't," he said.... I kept pushing him, "If you really want it, you can do it. You don't have to be the victim of time and money." At this point, I realized that I had become involved in a battle I was determined to win. He sensed my intensity and said, "Well, I'm just a simple journalist, and I guess I should be content with that." "No, you shouldn't," I said. "You should claim your deepest desire and do what you really want to do ... time and money aren't the real issue." "What is?" he asked. "You are," I answered. "You have nothing to lose. You are young, full of energy, well trained.... Everything is possible for you.... Why let the world squeeze you in? ... Why become a victim? You are free to do what you want — if, that is, you really want it!"

He looked at me with increasing surprise, wondering what it was that had gotten him into this bizarre conversation. "Well," he said, "I'd better go.... Maybe one day I will write my novel."

I stopped him, not wanting to let him off so easily.

"Wait, Fred, I meant what I said. Follow your desire." With a touch of sarcasm in his voice, he said, "Sounds good to me!" I didn't want to let him go. I realized that my own convictions were at stake. I believe that people can make choices and make them according to their own best aspirations. I also believe that people seldom make these choices. Instead, they blame the world, the society, and others for their "fate" and waste much of their life complaining. But I sensed, after our short verbal skirmish, that Fred was capable of jumping over his own fears and taking the risk of trusting himself. I knew also, however, that I had to jump first before he could, and so I said, "Fred, give up your job, come here for a year, and write your novel. I will get the money somehow."

Later — many years later — Fred told me that, when I said this, he got very nervous and began questioning my motives. "What does this man really want of me?" he thought. "Why is he offering me money and time to write? I don't trust this. There must be something else going on here!" But, instead of saying any of this, he only objected, "I am a Jew, and this is a Christian seminary." I pushed his objection aside. "We will make you a scholar in residence. . . . You can do what you like. . . . People here will love having a novelist in the house, and, meanwhile, you can learn something about Christianity and Judaism too."

A few months later, Fred came to Yale Divinity School and spent a year there trying to write his novel. It was never written, but we became close friends, and today, many years later, I am writing this book as a fruit of that friendship.

During the ten years or more that followed our time together at Yale, both Fred and I lived lives very different from what we anticipated when we first met. Fred lived through a very painful divorce; remarried; and now he and his wife, Robin, are expecting their first child. Meanwhile, he worked at different jobs, not very satisfying at first, until he found a position that offered him ample scope for the exercise of his creative abilities. My own journey was no more predictable. I left the academic world, went to Latin America, tried the academic world again and finally settled in a community with people who have a mental handicap and their assistants. There was much struggle, much pain, and much joy in both our lives, and we were able to share these experiences at length during regular visits. As time passed, we grew closer and became more and more aware of the importance of our friendship for each other, even though busyness, distance, and personal lifestyles often stood in the way of our seeing each other as much as we wanted.

From the very beginning of our friendship, we were quite conscious of our radically different religious backgrounds. At first, it seemed as if this would make it hard to support each other spiritually. Fred respected me as a Catholic priest and showed sincere interest in my life and work, but Christianity in general and the Catholic Church in particular were little more than one of his many objects of interest. For myself, I could quite easily understand Fred's secular Judaism, despite my feeling that he would gain much by growing closer to his own spiritual heritage. I vividly remember once telling Fred that it would be good for him to read the Hebrew Bible. He protested, "It doesn't speak to me. It is a strange far-away world...." "Well," I said, "read at least the Book of Qoheleth [Ecclesiastes], the one that opens with the words: 'Vanity of vanities.... All is vanity.'"

The next day Fred said, "I read it. . . . I never realized that there was a place for a skeptic in the Bible . . . one of my type. . . . That's very reassuring!" I remember thinking, "There is much more than a skeptic in you."

As we both grew older and became a little less concerned about success, career, fame, money, and time, questions of meaning and purpose came more into the center of our relationship.

In the midst of the many changes in our lives, both of us came into closer touch with our deeper desires. Different though our circumstances were, we both had to deal with the pains of rejection and separation, and both of us realized increasingly our desire for intimacy and friendship. To avoid being drowned in bitterness and resentment, we both had to draw on our deepest spiritual resources. Differences became less important, similarities more obvious. As our friendship grew deeper and stronger, our desire for a common spiritual foundation became more explicit.

One day, while walking on Columbus Avenue in New York City, Fred turned to me and said, "Why don't you write something about the spiritual life for me and my friends?" Fred was familiar with most of what I had written. Often he had given solid advice on form and style, but seldom did he feel connected with the content. As a Jew, living in the secular world of New York City, he couldn't find much comfort or support in words that were so explicitly Christian and so clearly based on a long life in the church. "It is good stuff," he often said, "but not for me." He felt strongly that his own experience and that of his friends required another tone, another language, another spiritual wavelength.

As I gradually came to know Fred's friends and got a feel for their interests and concerns, I better understood Fred's remarks about the need for a spirituality that speaks to men and women in a secularized society. Much of my thinking and writing presupposed a familiarity with concepts and images that for many centuries had nourished the spiritual life of Christians and Jews, but for many people these concepts and images had lost their power to bring them into touch with their spiritual center.

Fred's idea that I say something about the spirit that his friends and he "could hear" stayed with me. He was asking me to respond to the great spiritual hunger and thirst that exist in countless people who walk the streets of big cities. He was calling me to speak a word of hope to people who no longer came to churches or synagogues

"Why don't you write something about the spiritual life for me and my friends?"

and for whom priests and rabbis were no longer the obvious counselors.

"You have something to say," Fred kept telling me, "but you keep saying it to people who least need to hear it. . . . What about us young, ambitious, secular men and women wondering what life is all about after all? Can you speak to us with the same conviction as you speak to those who share your tradition, your language, and your vision?"

Fred was not the only one to ask me such questions. What Fred had expressed so clearly was coming at me from many other directions as well. I heard it from people in my community who had no religious background and for whom the Bible was a strange, confusing book. I heard it from members of my family who had long ago left the church and had no desire ever to return. I heard it from lawyers, doctors, and businessmen whose lives had taken up all their energy and for whom Saturday and Sunday were little more than a brief respite to gain enough strength to reenter the arena on Monday morning. I heard it, too, from young men and women beginning to feel the many demands of a society that claimed their attention, but fearing at the same time that it was not going to offer them much in the way of real life.

Fred's question became much more than the intriguing suggestion of a young New York intellectual. It became the plea that arose on all sides — wherever I was open to hear it. And, in the end, it became for me the most pertinent and the most urgent of all demands: "Speak to us about the deepest yearning of our hearts, about our many wishes, about hope; not about the many strategies for survival, but about trust; not about new methods of satisfying our emotional needs, but about love. Speak to us about a vision larger than our changing perspectives and about a voice deeper than the clamorings of our mass media. Yes, speak to us about something or someone greater than ourselves. Speak to us about . . . God."

"Who am I to speak about such things?" I answered. "My own life is too small for that. I don't have the experience, the knowledge or the language you are asking for. You and your friends live in a world so different from my own."

Fred didn't give me much room. "You can do it. . . . You have to do it. . . . If you don't, who will? . . . Visit me more often; talk to my friends; look attentively at what you see, and listen carefully to what you hear. You will discover a cry welling up from the depths of the human heart that has remained unheard because there was no one to listen."

Fred's words made me think of his apartment on 75th Street: a cozy place surrounded by a harsh world. When Fred first brought me there, many years ago, he drew my attention to the bareness of the building's entrance

23

hall. "Everything is stolen," he said. "The chandelier, the marble on the walls, whatever has any value is ripped off and taken, often in broad daylight." As the elevator took us to the eleventh floor, I felt an eerie silence among the passengers who were almost elbow to elbow. How close and yet how far apart. Fred needed two keys to open his apartment door, and he had to close tightly the double windows protected by iron bars to keep the noise of Columbus Avenue from invading every corner of his space. Yes, a pleasant home, but, when we finally found our way to it, a whole story of violence and oppression, fear and suspicion, anguish and agony, had already been told. There I learned about Fred's daily doings: leaving his apartment in the early morning and vanishing into the crowds on his way to work; reading the morning paper on the subway and working on a financial news-letter in a little office cubicle; taking his lunch with a colleague in a noisy restaurant, and spending the after-noon with countless phone calls and faxes, and then vanishing once again into the crowds, finding his way back to his cozy haven.

What could I possibly say to a man living in this kind

of place with this kind of rhythm? What could I possibly say to a world of rushing taxicabs, glass-covered office towers, and show business going on day and night? And still, wasn't I prepared during the many years of study, prayer, and encounters to be able to speak words of hope to precisely this world?

"But how? How?" I said to Fred, while feeling resistance and my eagerness to respond locked in an inner battle. His answer: "Speak from that place in your heart where you are most yourself. Speak directly, simply, lovingly, gently, and without any apologies. Tell us what you see and want us to see; tell us what you hear and want us to hear. . . . Trust your own heart. The words will come. There is nothing to fear. Those who need you most will help you most. You can be sure that I will."

And now, as I begin at last to write, I know that I can do so only when I stay very close to Fred and his friends. They called me to be who I want to be, but they gave me, as well, the assurance of their love.

I have chosen to speak directly — as I would in a personal letter. By keeping Fred and his friends at the center of my attention, I can best express what is in my heart. I am not able to deal with all the burning issues of our time and society, but I am able to write to a dear friend whom I came to know and love as a fellow-traveler searching for life, light, and truth. I hope that through my being so personal and direct many may want to "listen in" and even join in this spiritual search.

Being the Beloved

EVER SINCE YOU ASKED ME to write for you and your friends about the spiritual life, I have been wondering if there might be one word I would most want you to remember when you finished reading all I wish to say. Over the past year, that special word has gradually emerged from the depths of my own heart. It is the word "Beloved," and I am convinced that it has been given to me for the sake of you and your friends. Being a Christian, I first learned this word from the story of the baptism of Jesus of Nazareth. "No sooner had Jesus come up out of the water than he saw the heavens torn apart and the Spirit, like a dove, descending on him. And a voice came from heaven: 'You are my Son, the Beloved; my favor rests on you'" (Matt. 3:16–17; Mark 1:10–11; Luke 3:21–22). For many years I had read these words and even reflected upon them in sermons and lectures, but it is only since our talks in New York that they have taken on a meaning far beyond the boundaries of my own tradition. Our many conversations led me to the inner conviction that the words "You are my Beloved" revealed the most intimate truth about all human beings, whether they belong to any particular tradition or not.

Fred, all I want to say to you is "You are the Beloved," and all I hope is that you can hear these words as spoken to you with all the tenderness and force that love can hold. My only desire is to make these words reverberate in every corner of your being — "You are the Beloved."

The greatest gift my friendship can give to you is the gift of your Belovedness. I can give that gift only insofar as I have claimed it for myself. Isn't that what friendship is all about: giving to each other the gift of our Belovedness?

Yes, there is that voice, the voice that speaks from

above and from within and that whispers softly or de-
clares loudly: "You are my Beloved, on you my favor
rests." It certainly is not easy to hear that voice in a
world filled with voices that shout: "You are no good,

Isn't that what friendship is all about: giving to each other the gift of our Belovedness?

you are ugly; you are worthless; you are despicable, you
are nobody — unless you can demonstrate the opposite."

These negative voices are so loud and so persistent
that it is easy to believe them. That's the great trap. It
is the trap of self-rejection. Over the years, I have come
to realize that the greatest trap in our life is not success,
popularity, or power, but self-rejection. Success, popularity, and power can, indeed, present a great temptation,
but their seductive quality often comes from the way they
are part of the much larger temptation to self-rejection.

31

When we have come to believe in the voices that call us worthless and unlovable, then success, popularity, and power are easily perceived as attractive solutions. The real trap, however, is self-rejection. I am constantly surprised at how quickly I give in to this temptation. As soon as someone accuses me or criticizes me, as soon as I am rejected, left alone, or abandoned, I find myself thinking: "Well, that proves once again that I am a nobody." Instead of taking a critical look at the circumstances or trying to understand my own and others' limitations, I tend to blame myself — not just for what I did, but for who I am. My dark side says: "I am no good. . . . I deserve to be pushed aside, forgotten, rejected, and abandoned."

Maybe you think that you are more tempted by arrogance than by self-rejection. But isn't arrogance, in fact, the other side of self-rejection? Isn't arrogance putting yourself on a pedestal to avoid being seen as you see yourself? Isn't arrogance, in the final analysis, just another way of dealing with the feelings of worthlessness? Both self-rejection and arrogance pull us out of the common reality of existence and make a gentle community of people extremely difficult, if not impossible, to attain.

I know too well that beneath my arrogance there lies much self-doubt, just as there is a great amount of pride hidden in my self-rejection. Whether I am inflated or deflated, I lose touch with my truth and distort my vision of reality.

I hope you can somehow identify in yourself the temptation to self-rejection, whether it manifests itself in arrogance or in low self-esteem. Not seldom, self-rejection is simply seen as the neurotic expression of an insecure person. But neurosis is often the psychic manifestation of a much deeper human darkness: the darkness of not feeling truly welcome in human existence. Self-rejection is the greatest enemy of the spiritual life because it contradicts the sacred voice that calls us the "Beloved." Being the Beloved expresses the core truth of our existence.

I am putting this so directly and so simply because, though the experience of being the Beloved has never been completely absent from my life, I never claimed it as my core truth. I kept running around it in large or small circles, always looking for someone or something able to convince me of my Belovedness. It was as if I

Aren't you, like me, hoping that some person, thing, or event will come along to give you that final feeling of inner well-being you desire?

kept refusing to hear the voice that speaks from the very depth of my being and says: "You are my Beloved, on you my favor rests." That voice has always been there, but it seems that I was much more eager to listen to other, louder voices saying: "Prove that you are worth something; do something relevant, spectacular, or powerful, and then you will earn the love you so desire." Meanwhile, the soft, gentle voice that speaks in the silence and solitude of my heart remained unheard or, at least, unconvincing.

That soft, gentle voice that calls me the Beloved has come to me in countless ways. My parents, friends, teachers, students, and the many strangers who crossed my path have all sounded that voice in different tones. I have been cared for by many people with much tenderness and gentleness. I have been taught and instructed with much patience and perseverance. I have been encouraged to keep going when I was ready to give up and was stimulated to try again when I failed. I have been rewarded and praised for success...but, somehow, all of these signs of love were not sufficient to convince me that I was the Beloved. Beneath all my seemingly strong self-confidence there remained the question: "If all those who shower me with so much attention could see me and know me in my innermost self, would they still love me?" That agonizing question, rooted in my inner shadow, kept persecuting me and made me run away from the very place where that quiet voice calling me the Beloved could be heard.

I think you understand what I am talking about. Aren't you, like me, hoping that some person, thing, or event will come along to give you that final feeling of inner well-being you desire? Don't you often hope: "May this book, idea, course, trip, job, country, or relationship fulfill my deepest desire." But as long as you are waiting for that mysterious moment you will go on running helter-skelter, always anxious and restless, always lustful and angry, never fully satisfied. You know that this is the compulsiveness that keeps us going and busy, but at the same time makes us wonder whether we are getting anywhere in the long run. This is the way to spiritual exhaustion and burn-out. This is the way to spiritual death.

Well, you and I don't have to kill ourselves. We are the Beloved. We are intimately loved long before our parents, teachers, spouses, children, and friends loved or wounded us. That's the truth of our lives. That's the truth I want you to claim for yourself. That's the truth spoken by the voice that says, "You are my Beloved."

Listening to that voice with great inner attentiveness, I hear at my center words that say: "I have called you by name, from the very beginning. You are mine and I am yours. You are my Beloved, on you my favor rests. I have molded you in the depths of the earth and knitted you together in your mother's womb. I have carved you in the palms of my hands and hidden you in the shadow of my embrace. I look at you with infinite tenderness and care for you with a care more intimate than that of a mother for her child. I have counted every hair on your head and guided you at every step. Wherever you go, I go with you, and wherever you rest, I keep watch. I will give you food that will satisfy all your hunger and drink that will quench all your thirst. I will not hide my face from you. You know me as your own as I know you as my own. You belong to me. I am your father, your mother, your brother, your sister, your lover, and your spouse . . . yes, even your child . . . wherever you are I will be. Nothing will ever separate us. We are one."

Every time you listen with great attentiveness to the voice that calls you the Beloved, you will discover within yourself a desire to hear that voice longer and more deeply. It is like discovering a well in the desert. Once you have touched wet ground, you want to dig deeper.

I have been doing a lot of digging lately and I know that I am just beginning to see a little stream bubbling up through the dry sand. I have to keep digging because that little stream comes from a huge reservoir beneath the desert of my life. The word "digging" might not be the best word, since it suggests hard and painful work that finally leads me to the place where I can quench my thirst. Perhaps all we need to do is remove the dry sand that covers the well. There may be quite a pile of dry sand in our lives, but the One who so desires to quench our thirst will help us to remove it. All we really need is a great desire to find the water and drink from it.

You have lived fewer years than I. You may still want to look around a little more and a little longer so as to become convinced that the spiritual life is worth all your energy. But I do feel a certain impatience toward you because I don't want you to waste too much of your time! I have fewer years ahead of me than behind me. For you, I hope the opposite is true. Therefore, I want to assure you already, now, that you do not have to get caught in searches that lead only to entanglement. Neither do you have to become the victim of a manipulative world or get trapped in any kind of addiction. You can choose to reach out now to true inner freedom and find it ever more fully.

So, if you are interested in starting on the journey of the Beloved, I have a lot more to say to you, because the journey of the spiritual life calls not only for determination, but also for a certain knowledge of the terrain to be crossed. I don't want you to have to wander about in the desert for forty years as did our spiritual forebears. I don't even want you to dwell there as long as I did. You are very dear to me, a friend whom I truly love. Although it remains true that everyone has to learn for himself or herself, I still believe that we can prevent those we love from making the same mistakes we did. In the terrain of the spiritual life, we need guides. In the pages that I now want to write for you, I would like to be your guide. I hope you are still interested in walking along.

Becoming the Beloved

Enfleshing the Truth

DEAR FRIEND, being the Beloved is the origin and the fulfillment of the life of the Spirit. I say this because, as soon as we catch a glimpse of this truth, we are put on a journey in search of the fullness of that truth and we will not rest until we can rest in that truth. From the moment we claim the truth of being the Beloved, we are faced with the call to become who we are. Becoming the Beloved is the great spiritual journey we have to make.

Augustine's words, "My soul is restless until it rests in you, O God," capture well this journey. I know that the fact that I am always searching for God, always struggling to discover the fullness of Love, always yearning for the complete truth, tells me that I have already been given a taste of God, of Love, and of Truth. I can only look for something that I have, to some degree, already found. How can I search for beauty and truth unless that beauty and truth are already known to me in the depth of my heart? It seems that all of us human beings have deep inner memories of the paradise that we have lost. Maybe the word "innocence" is better than the word "paradise." We were innocent before we started feeling guilty; we were in the light before we entered into the darkness; we were at home before we started to search for a home. Deep in the recesses of our minds and hearts there lies hidden the treasure we seek. We know its preciousness, and we know that it holds the gift we most desire: a life stronger than death.

If it is true that we not only are the Beloved, but also have to *become* the Beloved; if it is true that we not only *are* children of God, but also have to *become* children of

44

God; if it is true that we not only *are* brothers and sisters, but also have to *become* brothers and sisters . . . if all that is true, how then can we get a grip on this process of becoming? If the spiritual life is not simply a way of being, but also a way of becoming, what then is the nature of this becoming?

You are enough of a pragmatist to ask how we get from the first to the second innocence, from the first to the second childhood, from being the Beloved to fully becoming it. This is such an important question because it forces us to let go of any romanticism or idealism and to deal with the utter concreteness of our daily lives. *Becoming the Beloved means letting the truth of our Belovedness become enfleshed in everything we think, say, or do.* It entails a long and painful process of appropriation or, better, incarnation. As long as "being the Beloved" is little more than a beautiful thought or a lofty idea that hangs above my life to keep me from becoming depressed, nothing really changes. What is required is to become the Beloved in the commonplaces of my daily existence and, bit by bit, to close the gap that exists between what I know myself to be and the countless specific realities of everyday life. Becoming the Beloved is pulling the truth revealed to me from above down into the ordinariness of what I am, in fact, thinking of, talking about, and doing from hour to hour.

When I think about your life and the lives of Robin and your friends, I am quite aware of the pressures you undergo. You and Robin live in the middle of New York in a small apartment; you have to keep working to earn enough for your rent and your food; you have thousands of little things to do, from making phone calls to writing letters, buying and cooking food, staying in touch with family and friends and remaining informed about what happens in your city, your country, and your world. All of that seems quite a lot for one person, and it is usually these very simple concrete things of daily living that provide the raw materials for our conversations. The question, "How are you doing?" usually leads to very down-to-earth stories about marriage, family, health, work, money, friends, and plans for the immediate future. It seldom, however, leads to deep thoughts about the origin and goal of our existence. Still, I am thoroughly convinced that the origin and goal of our existence have everything to do with the ways we think, talk, and act in our daily lives. When our deepest truth is that we are the Beloved and when our greatest joy and peace come from fully claiming that truth, it follows that this has to become visible and tangible in the ways we eat and drink, talk and love, play and work. When the deepest currents of our life no longer have any influence on the waves at the surface, then our vitality will eventually ebb, and we will end up listless and bored even when we are busy.

So, my task now is to write about that process of becoming the Beloved as it can be pinpointed in our very concrete daily lives. What I will attempt to describe are the movements of the Spirit as they take place within us and around us. As you know, we live in a very "psychological" age. We know a lot about our emotions, passions, and feelings. We are quite aware of the many connections between our early experiences and our present behaviors. We have become quite sophisticated about our own psychosexual development and can easily identify our moments of victimization and our moments of real freedom. We know about being defensive; we know about projecting our own needs and fears onto others, and we know that our self-doubts can easily get in the way of our creativity. My question is whether it is possible to be as articulate about our spiritual journey as we are about our psychological journey. Can we come into touch with that mysterious process of becoming the Beloved in the same specific way as we can come into touch with the "dynamics" of our psyches?

You may wonder if psychodynamics are really so different from the movements of the Spirit. I think they are, even though they connect and intersect in many ways. What I want to describe is how the movements of the Spirit of love manifest themselves in our daily struggles and how we can develop disciplines to identify these movements and respond to them in our actions.

To identify the movements of the Spirit in our lives, I have found it helpful to use four words: "taken," "blessed," "broken," and "given." These words summarize my life as a priest because each day, when I come together around the table with members of my community, I take bread, bless it, break it, and give it. These words also summarize my life as a Christian because, as a Christian, I am

To identify the movements of the Spirit in our lives, I have found it helpful to use four words: "taken," "blessed," "broken," and "given."

called to become bread for the world: bread that is taken, blessed, broken, and given. Most importantly, however, they summarize my life as a human being because in every moment of my life somewhere, somehow the taking, the blessing, the breaking, and the giving are happening.

I must tell you at this point that these four words have become the most important words of my life. Only gradually has their meaning become known to me, and I feel that I won't ever know their full profundity. They are the most personal as well as the most universal words. They express the most spiritual as well as the most secular truth. They speak about the most divine as well as the most human behavior. They reach high as well as low, embrace God as well as all people. They succinctly express the complexity of life and embrace its ever-unfolding mystery. They are the keys to understanding not only the lives of the great prophets of Israel and the life of Jesus of Nazareth, but also our own lives. I have chosen them not only because they are so deeply engraved in my being, but also because, through them, I have come into touch with the ways of becoming the Beloved of God.

TAKEN

To become the Beloved we, first of all, have to claim that we are taken. That might sound very strange at first, and, still, to be taken is essential in becoming the Beloved. As I have mentioned already, we can desire to become the Beloved only when we know that we already are the Beloved. Therefore, the first step in the spiritual life is to acknowledge with our whole being that we already have been taken.

It might help at this point if, instead of "take," which is a somewhat cold and brittle word, we used a warmer, softer word with the same meaning: the word "choose." As children of God, we are God's chosen ones.

I hope that the word "chosen" speaks to you. It must be for you a word with very special connotations. As a Jew, you know the positive and the negative associations in being considered one of God's chosen people.

You often told me about the rich heritage of your family, the deep faith of your grandparents, and the many traditions that connected your parents with the sacred history of your people. But you also told me about the cruel pogroms in the "old" country and the long and painful journey that brought your mother and father to America. Although you yourself have not suffered directly from persecution, you are quite aware of how much it is part

When I know that I am chosen, I know that I have been seen as a special person.

of your story and how frighteningly close it is to the surface of your life. You showed me that anti-Semitism is always lurking around in one form or another, and recent events, both in Europe and in the United States, only confirm your conviction that "blaming the Jews" is not something of the past. I wouldn't be surprised if a part of you protests against the idea of being chosen. I recognize this in my own life. Being an ordained priest, I was often treated as a special person, as "set aside," as chosen to be different. Often I have tried to show or to prove that I was "just me" (one way to explain the "J. M." in my name!) and that I had no desire to be put on a pedestal and treated as a special person. I sensed, as you obviously do, that when you are treated as the chosen one, you are as liable to be persecuted as admired.

Still, I do believe deeply that, in order to live a spiritual life, we have to claim for ourselves that we are "taken" or "chosen." Let me try to expand a bit on these words. When I know that I am chosen, I know that I have been seen as a special person. Someone has noticed me in my uniqueness and has expressed a desire to know me, to come closer to me, to love me. When I write to you that, as the Beloved, we are God's chosen ones, I mean that we have been seen by God from all eternity and seen as unique, special, precious beings. It is very hard for me to express well the depth of meaning the word "chosen" has for me, but I hope you are willing to listen to me from within. From all eternity, long before you were born and became a part of history, you existed in God's heart. Long before your parents admired you or your friends acknowledged your gifts or your teachers, colleagues, and employers encouraged you, you were already "chosen." The eyes of love had seen you as precious, as of infinite beauty, as of eternal value. When love chooses, it chooses with a perfect sensitivity for the unique beauty of the chosen one, and it chooses without making anyone else feel excluded.

We touch here a great spiritual mystery: To be chosen does not mean that others are rejected. It is very hard to conceive of this in a competitive world such as ours. All my memories of being chosen are linked to memories of others not being chosen. When I was not chosen for a soccer team, not chosen to be the leader of the Boy Scout patrol, or when I was chosen to be the "senior" of my ordination class, or to be honored with special awards, there were always tears alongside smiles and smiles alongside tears. Competition and comparison were always there. How often I needed the words: "The fact that you are not chosen does not mean that you are not good, only that someone else is a little better."

But even these words were seldom consoling because the feeling of rejection was always there. And when I was chosen and selected as the best, I was always aware of how disappointed others were at not being in my place. It was then that I needed to hear the words: "The fact that you are chosen does not mean that others are not good, only that you are a little better." But, again, these words did not help very much because I was unable to make the others feel as happy as I. In this world, to be chosen simply means to be set apart in contrast to others. You know how in our extremely competitive society the "chosen ones" are looked at with special attention. Whole magazines are dedicated to "heroes" of sport, film, music, acting, and other ways of excelling. They are the "chosen ones" and their devotees, whether readers, listeners, or viewers, try to extract some vicarious pleasure from knowing them or being close to them.

To be chosen as the Beloved of God is something radically different. Instead of excluding others, it includes others. Instead of rejecting others as less valuable, it accepts others in their own uniqueness. It is not a competitive, but a compassionate choice. Our minds have great difficulty in coming to grips with such a reality. Maybe our minds will never understand it. Perhaps it is only our hearts that can accomplish this. Every time we hear about "chosen people," "chosen talents," or "chosen friends," we almost automatically start thinking about elites and find ourselves not far from feelings of jealousy, anger, or resentment. Not seldom has the perception of others as being chosen led to aggression, violence, and war.

But I beg you, do not surrender the word "chosen" to the world. Dare to claim it as your own, even when it is constantly misunderstood. You must hold on to the truth that you are the chosen one. That truth is the bedrock on which you can build a life as the Beloved. When you lose touch with your chosenness, you expose yourself to the temptation of self-rejection, and that temptation undermines the possibility of ever growing as the Beloved.

As I look within as well as around myself, I am overwhelmed by the dark voices telling me, "You are nothing special; you are just another person among millions; your life is just one more mouth to feed; your needs just one more problem to solve." These voices are increasingly powerful, especially in a time marked by so many broken relationships. Many children never feel really welcomed in the world. Beneath their nervous smiles, there is often the question: "Am I really wanted?" Some young people even hear their mothers say: "I hadn't really expected you, but once I found out I was pregnant I decided to have you anyway.... You were sort of an accident." Words or attitudes such as these do nothing to make a person feel "chosen." Our world is full of people who question whether it would have been better had they not been born. When we do not feel loved by those who gave us life, we often suffer our whole life long from a low self-esteem that can lead easily to depression, despair, and even suicide.

In the midst of this extremely painful reality, we have to dare to reclaim the truth that we are God's chosen ones, even when our world does not choose us. As long as we allow our parents, siblings, teachers, friends, and lovers to determine whether we are chosen or not, we are caught in the net of a suffocating world that accepts or rejects us according to its own agenda of effectiveness and control. Often this reclaiming is an arduous task, a lifelong work because the world persists in its efforts to pull us into the darkness of self-doubt, low self-esteem, self-rejection, and depression. And this because it is as insecure, fearful, self-deprecating people that we can most easily be used and manipulated by the powers surrounding us. The great spiritual battle begins — and never ends — with the reclaiming of our chosenness. Long before any human being saw us, we are seen by God's loving eyes. Long before anyone heard us cry or laugh, we are heard by our God who is all ears for us. Long before any person spoke to us in this world, we are spoken to by the voice of eternal love. Our preciousness, uniqueness, and individuality are not given to us by those who meet us in clock-time — our brief chronological existence — but by the One who has chosen us with an everlasting love, a love that existed from all eternity and will last through all eternity.

How do we get in touch with our chosenness when we are surrounded by rejections? I have already said that this involves a real spiritual struggle. Are there any guidelines in this struggle? Let me try to formulate a few.

First of all, you have to keep unmasking the world about you for what it is: manipulative, controlling, power-hungry, and, in the long run, destructive. The world tells you many lies about who you are, and you simply have to be realistic enough to remind yourself of this. Every time

We are God's chosen ones, even when our world does not choose us.

you feel hurt, offended, or rejected, you have to dare to say to yourself: "These feelings, strong as they may be, are not telling me the truth about myself. The truth, even though I cannot feel it right now, is that I am the chosen child of God, precious in God's eyes, called the Beloved from all eternity, and held safe in an everlasting embrace."

Second, you have to keep looking for people and places where your truth is spoken and where you are reminded of your deepest identity as the chosen one. Yes, we must dare to opt consciously for our chosenness and not allow our emotions, feelings, or passions to seduce us into self-rejection. The synagogues, the churches, the many communities of faith, the different support groups helping us with our addictions, family, friends, teachers, and students: All of these can become reminders of our truth. The limited, sometimes broken, love of those who share our humanity can often point us to the truth of who we are: precious in God's eyes. This truth is not simply an inner truth that emerges from our center. It is also a truth that is revealed to us by the One who has chosen us. That is why we have to keep listening to the many men and women in history who, through their lives and their words, call us back to it.

Third, you have to celebrate your chosenness constantly. This means saying "thank you" to God for having chosen you, and "thank you" to all who remind you of your chosenness. Gratitude is the most fruitful way of deepening your consciousness that you are not an "accident," but a divine choice. It is important to realize how often we have had chances to be grateful and have not used them. When someone is kind to us, when an event turns out well, when a problem is solved, a relationship restored, a wound healed, there are very concrete reasons to offer thanks: be it with words, with flowers, with a letter, a card, a phone call, or just a gesture of affection. However, precisely the same situations also offer us occasions to be critical, skeptical, even cynical because, when someone is kind to us, we can question his or her motives; when an event turns out well, it could always have turned out better; when a problem is solved, there often emerges another in its place; when a relationship is restored, there is always the question: "For how long?"; when a wound is healed, there still can be some leftover pain. . . . Where there is reason for gratitude, there can always be found a reason for bitterness. It is here that we are faced with the freedom to make a decision. We can decide to be grateful or to be bitter. We can decide to recognize our chosenness in the moment or we can decide to focus on the shadow side. When we persist in looking at the shadow side, we will eventually end up in the dark. I see this every day in our community. The core members, the men and women with mental disabilities, have many reasons to be bitter. Many of them experience deep loneliness, rejection from family members or friends, the unfulfilled desire to have a partner in life, and the constant frustration of always needing assistance. Still, they choose mostly not to be bitter, but grateful for the many small gifts of their lives — for an invitation to dinner, for a few days of retreat or a birthday celebration, and, most of all, for their daily life in community with people who offer friendship and support. They choose gratitude over bitterness and they become a great source of hope and inspiration for all their assistants who, although not mentally disabled, also have to make that same choice. When we keep claiming the light, we will find ourselves becoming more and more radiant. What fascinates me so much is that every time we decide to be grateful it will be easier to see new things to be grateful for. Gratitude begets gratitude, just as love begets love.

I hope that these three guidelines for getting in touch with your chosenness can help you in your daily life. For me, they are the spiritual disciplines for my life as the chosen one. It is not easy to practice them, especially during times of crisis. Before I know it, I find myself complaining again, brooding again about some rejection and plotting ways to take revenge, but, when I keep my disciplines close to my heart, I am able to step over my shadow into the light of my truth.

Before concluding these thoughts about "being chosen," I want to impress upon you the importance of this truth for our relationships with others. When we claim and constantly reclaim the truth of being the chosen

When we keep claiming the light, we will find ourselves becoming more and more radiant.

ones, we soon discover within ourselves a deep desire to reveal to others their own chosenness. Instead of making us feel that we are better, more precious or valuable than others, our awareness of being chosen opens our eyes to the chosenness of others. That is the great joy of being chosen: the discovery that others are chosen as well. In the house of God there are many mansions. There is a place for everyone — a unique, special place. Once we deeply trust that we ourselves are precious in God's eyes, we are able to recognize the preciousness of others and their unique places in God's heart. This makes me think of Helen, one of the handicapped members of our community. When she came to Daybreak a few years ago, I felt quite distant from her, even a bit afraid. She lived in a little world of her own, only uttering distracting noises and never making any personal contact. But as we came to know her better and trusted that she, too, has a unique gift to offer, she gradually came out of her isolation, started to smile at us, and became a great source of joy for the whole community.

I now realize that I had to be in touch with my own goodness to discover the unique goodness of Helen. As long as my self-doubts and fears guided me, I couldn't create the space for Helen to reveal to me her beauty. But once I claimed my own chosenness, I could be with Helen as a person who had much, very much, to offer me. It is impossible to compete for God's love. God's love is a love that includes all people — each one in his or her uniqueness. It is only when we have claimed our own place in God's love that we can experience this all-embracing, noncomparing love and feel safe, not only with God, but also with all our brothers and sisters.

You and I know how true to life this all is. We have been friends now for many years. In the beginning there was some comparing, some jealousy, some competition. But as we grew older and became more sure in our own uniqueness, most, if not all, of this rivalry vanished, and we were more able to affirm and call forth each other's gifts. I feel so good being with you because I know that you enjoy me for who I am and not just for what I can do for you. And you feel good when I come to visit you because you know that I marvel in your kindness, your goodness, and your many gifts — not because they prove helpful for me, but simply because of you. Deep friendship is a calling forth of each other's chosenness and a mutual affirmation of being precious in God's eyes. Your life and my life are, each of them, one of a kind. No one has lived your life or my life before, and no one will ever live them again. Our lives are unique stones in the mosaic of human existence — priceless and irreplaceable.

Being chosen is the basis for being the Beloved. It is a lifelong struggle to claim that chosenness, but also a lifelong joy. The more fully we claim it, the more easily will we also discover another aspect of being the Beloved: our blessedness. Let me speak to you about that now.

BLESSED

As the Beloved Children of God, we are blessed. The word "blessing" has become very important for me over the past few years, and you are one of the friends who made it important for me.

Do you remember how one Saturday morning in New York City you took me to the synagogue? When we arrived, we discovered that there was to be a bar mitzvah. A young man, thirteen years old, was declared adult by his congregation. For the first time, he gave leadership to the service. He read from the Book of Genesis and gave a short sermon about the importance of caring for our environment. He was affirmed by the rabbi and his friends and blessed by his parents. It was the first time that I had witnessed a bar mitzvah, and I was deeply moved — most of all by the parents' blessing. I still hear the father saying: "Son, whatever will happen to you in your life, whether you will have success or not, become important or not, will be healthy or not, always remember how much your mother and I love you." When he said this in front of the congregation, looking gently at the boy standing before him, tears came to my eyes, and I thought: "What a grace such a blessing is."

I am increasingly aware of how much we fearful, anxious, insecure human beings are in need of a blessing. Children need to be blessed by their parents and parents by their children. We all need each other's blessings — masters and disciples, rabbis and students, bishops and priests, doctors and patients.

Let me first tell you what I mean by the word "blessing." In Latin, to bless is *benedicere.* The word "benediction" that is used in many churches means literally: speaking (*dictio*) well (*bene*) or saying good things of someone. That speaks to me. I need to hear good things said of me, and I know how much you have the same need. Nowadays, we often say: "We have to affirm each other." Without affirmation, it is hard to live well. To give someone a blessing is the most significant affirmation we can offer. It is more than a word of praise or apprecia-

To give someone a blessing is the most significant affirmation we can offer.

tion; it is more than pointing out someone's talents or good deeds; it is more than putting someone in the light. To give a blessing is to affirm, to say "yes" to a person's Belovedness. And more than that: To give a blessing creates the reality of which it speaks. There is a lot of mutual admiration in this world, just as there is a lot of mutual condemnation. A blessing goes beyond the distinction between admiration or condemnation, between virtues or vices, between good deeds or evil deeds. A blessing touches the original goodness of the other and calls forth his or her Belovedness.

Not long ago, in my own community, I had a very personal experience of the power of a real blessing. Shortly before I started a prayer service in one of our houses, Janet, a handicapped member of our community, said to me: "Henri, can you give me a blessing?" I responded in a somewhat automatic way by tracing with my thumb the sign of the cross on her forehead. Instead of being grateful, however, she protested vehemently, "No, that doesn't work. I want a real blessing!" I suddenly became aware of the ritualistic quality of my response to her request and said, "Oh, I am sorry, . . . let me give you a real blessing when we are all together for the prayer service." She nodded with a smile, and I realized that something special was required of me. After the service, when about thirty people were sitting in a circle on the floor, I said, "Janet has asked me for a special blessing. She feels that she needs that now." As I was saying this, I didn't know what Janet really wanted. But Janet didn't leave me in doubt for very long. As soon as I had said, "Janet has asked me for a special blessing," she stood up and walked toward me. I was wearing a long white robe with ample sleeves covering my hands as well as my arms. Spontaneously, Janet put her arms around me and put her head against my chest. Without thinking, I covered her with my sleeves so that she almost vanished in the folds of my robe. As we held each other, I said, "Janet, I want you to know that you are God's Beloved Daughter. You are precious in God's eyes. Your beautiful smile, your kindness to the people in your house, and all the good things you do show us what a beautiful human being you are. I know you feel a little low these days and that there is some sadness in your heart, but I want you to remember who you are: a very special person, deeply loved by God and all the people who are here with you."

As I said these words, Janet raised her head and looked at me; and her broad smile showed that she had really heard and received the blessing. When she returned to her place, Jane, another handicapped woman, raised her hand and said, "I want a blessing too." She stood up and, before I knew it, had put her face against my chest. After I had spoken words of blessing to her, many more of the handicapped people followed, expressing the same desire to be blessed. The most touching moment, however, came when one of the assistants, a twenty-four-year-old student, raised his hand and said, "And what about me?" "Sure," I said. "Come." He came, and, as we stood before each other, I put my arms around him and said, "John, it is so good that you are here. You are God's

Beloved Son. Your presence is a joy for all of us. When things are hard and life is burdensome, always remember that you are loved with an everlasting love." As I spoke these words, he looked at me with tears in his eyes and then he said, "Thank you, thank you very much."

That evening I recognized the importance of blessing and being blessed and reclaimed it as a true sign of the Beloved. The blessings that we give to each other are expressions of the blessing that rests on us from all eternity. It is the deepest affirmation of our true self. It is not enough to be chosen. We also need an ongoing blessing that allows us to hear in an ever-new way that we belong to a loving God who will never leave us alone, but will remind us always that we are guided by love on every step of our lives. Abraham and Sarah, Isaac and Rebecca, Jacob, Leah and Rachel, they all heard that blessing and so became the fathers and mothers of our faith. They lived their long and often painful journeys without ever forgetting that they were the blessed ones. Jesus, too, heard that blessing after John the Baptist had baptized him in the Jordan. A voice came from heaven saying: "You are my Beloved Son, on you my favor rests." This was a blessing, and it was that blessing that sustained Jesus through all the praise and blame, admiration and condemnation that followed. Like Abraham and Sarah, Jesus never lost the intimate knowledge that he was "the blessed one."

I tell you all of this because I know how moody you and I can be. One day we feel great, the next we feel miserable. One day we are full of new ideas, the next everything looks bleak and dull. One day we think we can take on the whole world, but the next even a little request seems too much for us. These mood swings show that we no longer hear the blessing that was heard by Abraham and Sarah, Isaac and Rebecca, Jacob, Leah and Rachel, and Jesus of Nazareth and that we, too, are to hear. When we are thrown up and down by the little waves on the surface of our existence, we become easy victims of our manipulative world, but, when we continue to hear the deep gentle voice that blesses us, we can walk through life with a stable sense of well-being and true belonging.

The feeling of being blessed is not, it seems to me, the feeling that we generally have about ourselves. You have lived many hard moments in your life, moments in which you felt more cursed than blessed. And I can say the same. In fact, I suspect that many people suffer from a deep sense of being cursed. When I simply listen to what people talk about during dinner, in restaurants, during work breaks, I hear much — much blaming and complaining in a spirit of passive resignation. Many people, and we too at times, feel like victims of a world we cannot change, and the daily newspapers certainly don't help much in coping with that feeling. The sense of being cursed often comes more easily than the sense of being blessed, and we can find enough arguments to feed it. We can say: "Look at what is happening in the world: Look at the starving people, the refugees, the prisoners, the sick and the dying. . . . Look at all the poverty, injustice and war. . . . Look at the torture, the killings, the destruction of nature and culture. . . . Look at our daily struggles with our relationships, with our work, with our health. . . . " Where, where is the blessing? The feeling of being accursed comes easily. We easily hear an inner voice calling us evil, bad, rotten, worthless, useless, doomed to sickness and death. Isn't it easier for us to believe that we are cursed than that we are blessed?

Still, I say to you, as the Beloved Son of God, you are blessed. Good words are being spoken to you and about you — words that tell the truth. The curses — noisy, boisterous, loud-mouthed as they may be — do not tell the truth. They are lies; lies easy to believe, but lies nevertheless.

Well, if the blessing speaks the truth and the curse speaks lies about who you and I are, we are faced with the very concrete question: How to hear and claim the blessing? If the fact of our blessedness is not just a sentiment, but a truth that shapes our daily lives, we must be able to see and experience this blessing in an unambiguous way. Let me offer you two suggestions for claiming your blessedness. These have to do with prayer and presence.

First of all, prayer. For me personally, prayer becomes more and more a way to listen to the blessing. I have read and written much about prayer, but when I go to a quiet place to pray, I realize that, although I have a tendency to say many things to God, the real "work" of prayer is to become silent and listen to the voice that says good things about me. This might sound self-indulgent, but, in practice, it is a hard discipline. I am so afraid of being cursed, of hearing that I am no good or not

The real "work" of prayer is to become silent and listen to the voice that says good things about me.

good enough, that I quickly give in to the temptation to start talking and to keep talking in order to control my fears. To gently push aside and silence the many voices that question my goodness and to trust that I will hear a voice of blessing — that demands real effort.

Have you ever tried to spend a whole hour doing nothing but listening to the voice that dwells deep in your heart? When there is no radio to listen to, no TV to watch, no book to read, no person to talk to, no project to finish, no phone call to make, how does that make you feel? Often it does no more than make us so aware of how much there is still to do that we haven't yet done that we decide to leave the fearful silence and go back to work! It is not easy to enter into the silence and reach beyond the many boisterous and demanding voices of our world and to discover there the small intimate voice saying: "You are my Beloved Child, on you my favor rests." Still, if we dare to embrace our solitude and befriend our silence, we will come to know that voice. I do not want to suggest to you that one day you will hear that voice with your bodily ears. I am not speaking about a hallucinatory voice, but about a voice that can be heard by the ear of faith, the ear of the inner heart.

Often you will feel that nothing happens in your prayer. You say: "I am just sitting there and getting distracted." But if you develop the discipline of spending one half-hour a day listening to the voice of love, you will gradually discover that something is happening of which you were not even conscious. It might be only in retrospect that you discover the voice that blesses you. You thought that what happened during your time of listening was nothing more than a lot of confusion, but then you discover yourself looking forward to your quiet time and missing it when you can't have it. The movement of God's Spirit is very gentle, very soft — and hidden. It does not seek attention. But that movement is also very persistent, strong and deep. It changes our hearts radically. The faithful discipline of prayer reveals to you that you are the blessed one and gives you the power to bless others.

It might be helpful to offer here a concrete suggestion. One good way to listen is to listen with a sacred text: a psalm or a prayer, for instance. The Hindu spiritual writer Eknath Easwaran showed me the great value of learning a sacred text by heart and repeating it slowly in the mind, word by word, sentence by sentence. In this way, listening to the voice of love becomes not just a passive waiting, but an active attentiveness to the voice that speaks to us through the words of the Scriptures.

I spent many of my half-hours of prayer doing nothing but slowly repeating the prayer of St. Francis: "Lord make me an instrument of your peace. Where there is hatred let me show love...." As I let these words move from my mind to my heart, I began to experience, beyond all my restless emotions and feelings, the peace and love I was asking for in words.

In this way I also had a way to deal with my endless distractions. When I found myself wandering away far and wide, I could always return to my simple prayer and thereby listen again in my heart to the voice I so much wanted to hear.

My second suggestion for claiming your blessedness is the cultivation of presence. By presence I mean attentiveness to the blessings that come to you day after day, year after year. The problem of modern living is that we are too busy — looking for affirmation in the wrong places? — to notice that we are being blessed. Often, people say good things about us, but we brush them aside with remarks such as, "Oh, don't mention it, forget about it, it's nothing..." and so on. These remarks may seem to be expressions of humility, but they are, in fact, signs that we are not truly present to receive the blessings that are given. It is not easy for us, busy people, to truly receive a blessing. Perhaps the fact that few people offer a real blessing is the sad result of the absence of people who are willing and able to receive such a blessing. It

The problem of modern living is that we are too busy to notice that we are being blessed.

has become extremely difficult for us to stop, listen, pay attention, and receive gracefully what is offered to us.

Living with people who have a mental handicap makes this clear to me. They have many blessings to offer, but when I am forever busy, forever on the way to something important, how can I receive those blessings? Adam, one of the members of my community, cannot speak, cannot walk alone, cannot eat without help, cannot dress or undress himself, but he has great blessings to offer to those who take the time to be present to him, holding him or just sitting with him. I have yet to meet anyone who spent much time with Adam and didn't feel blessed by him. It is a blessing that comes from simple presence. But you know, too, how hard such simple presence is. There is always so much that still has to be done, so many tasks to finish and jobs to work on that simple presence can easily seem useless and even a waste of our time. But still, without a conscious desire to "waste" our time, it is hard to hear the blessing.

This attentive presence can allow us to see how many blessings there are for us to receive: the blessings of the poor who stop us on the road, the blessings of the blossoming trees and fresh flowers that tell us about new life, the blessings of music, painting, sculpture, and architecture — all of that — but most of all the blessings that come to us through words of gratitude, encouragement, affection, and love. These many blessings do not have to be invented. They are there, surrounding us on all sides. But we have to be present to them and receive them. They don't force themselves on us. They are gentle reminders of that beautiful, strong, but hidden, voice of the one who calls us by name and speaks good things about us.

Well, I truly hope that these two suggestions, prayer and presence, can help you to claim the blessedness that is yours. I cannot stress enough the importance of making this claim. Not claiming your blessedness will lead you quickly to the land of the cursed. There is little or no neutral territory between the land of the blessed and the land of the cursed. You have to choose where it is that you want to live, and that choice is one that you have to keep making from moment to moment.

Before concluding these thoughts about our being blessed, I must tell you that claiming your own blessedness always leads to a deep desire to bless others. The characteristic of the blessed ones is that, wherever they go, they always speak words of blessing. It is remarkable how easy it is to bless others, to speak good things to and about them, to call forth their beauty and truth, when you yourself are in touch with your own blessedness. The blessed one always blesses. And people want to be blessed! This is so apparent wherever you go. No one is brought to life through curses, gossip, accusations, or blaming. There is so much of that taking place around us all the time. And it calls forth only darkness, destruction and death. As the "blessed ones," we can walk through this world and offer blessings. It doesn't require much effort. It flows naturally from our hearts. When we hear within ourselves the voice calling us by name and blessing us, the darkness no longer distracts us. The voice that calls us the Beloved will give us words to bless others and reveal to them that they are no less blessed than we.

You live in New York. I live in Toronto. As you walk down Columbus Avenue and I down Yonge Street, we can have no illusions about the darkness. The loneliness, the homelessness, and the addictedness of people are all too visible. Yet all of these people yearn for a blessing. That blessing can be given only by those who have heard it themselves. I now feel ready to write to you about the hardest truth to put into words: the truth of our common brokenness. We are chosen and blessed. When we have truly owned this, have said "Yes" to it, then we can face our own and others' brokenness with open eyes. Let's do that now.

BROKEN

The moment has come to talk about our brokenness. You are a broken man. I am a broken man, and all the people we know or know about are broken. Our brokenness is so visible and tangible, so concrete and specific, that it is often difficult to believe that there is much to think, speak, or write about other than our brokenness.

From the moment we met, we spoke about our brokenness. You wanted something about me for the Connecticut section of the *New York Times*. I told you about my writing as a means of dealing with my loneliness, my sense of isolation, my many fears, and my general sense of insecurity. When the discussion shifted to you, you spoke of your discontent with your job, your frustration at not having enough time or money to write your own novel, and your general confusion as to the course of your life. In the year that followed our first encounter, we became increasingly open to each other about our suffering and pain. In fact, the sharing of our deep struggles became a sign of our friendship.

You had to live through a painful separation and divorce and I through a long period of depression. You had many disappointments in your work and kept wondering about your true calling in life, while I kept being overwhelmed by the many demands made on my time and energy that often lead me to exhaustion and despair.

Whenever we met again, we became more aware of the brokenness of our lives. There is nothing abnormal about this. When people come together they easily focus on their brokenness. The most-celebrated musical composition, the most-noted painting and sculpture, and the most-read books are often direct expressions of the human awareness of brokenness. This awareness is never far beneath the surface of our existence because we all know that none of us will escape death — the most radical manifestation of brokenness.

The leaders and prophets of Israel, who were clearly chosen and blessed, all lived very broken lives. And we, the Beloved Sons and Daughters of God, cannot escape our brokenness either.

There are many things I would like to say to you about our brokenness. But where to begin?

Perhaps the simplest beginning would be to say that our brokenness reveals something about who we are. Our sufferings and pains are not simply bothersome interruptions of our lives; rather, they touch us in our uniqueness and our most intimate individuality. The way I am broken tells you something unique about me. The way you are broken tells me something unique about you. That is the reason for my feeling very privileged when you freely share some of your deep pain with me, and that is why it is an expression of my trust in you when I disclose to you something of my vulnerable side. Our brokenness is always lived and experienced as highly personal, intimate and unique. I am deeply convinced that each human being suffers in a way no other human being suffers. No doubt, we can make comparisons; we can talk about more or less suffering, but, in the final analysis, your pain and my pain are so deeply personal that comparing them can bring scarcely any consolation or comfort. In fact, I am more grateful for a person who can acknowledge that I am very alone in my pain than for someone who tries to tell me that there are many others who have a similar or a worse pain.

Our brokenness is truly ours. Nobody else's. Our brokenness is as unique as our chosenness and our blessedness. The way we are broken is as much an expression of our individuality as the way we are taken and blessed. Yes, fearsome as it may sound, as the Beloved ones, we are called to claim our unique brokenness, just

Each human being suffers in a way no other human being suffers.

as we have to claim our unique chosenness and our unique blessedness.

I must try now to get a little closer to our experience of being broken. As I have said already, this is a very personal experience and, in the society in which you and I

live, it is generally an experience of inner brokenness —
a brokenness of the heart. Although many people suffer
from physical or mental disabilities, and although there is
a great amount of economic poverty, homelessness, and
lack of basic human needs, the suffering of which I am
most aware on a day-to-day basis is the suffering of the
broken heart. Again and again, I see the immense pain of
broken relationships between husbands and wives, parents and children, lovers, friends, and colleagues. In the
Western world, the suffering that seems to be the most
painful is that of feeling rejected, ignored, despised and
left alone. In my own community, with many severely
handicapped men and women, the greatest source of suffering is not the handicap itself, but the accompanying
feelings of being useless, worthless, unappreciated, and
unloved. It is much easier to accept the inability to speak,
walk, or feed oneself than it is to accept the inability to
be of special value to another person. We human beings
can suffer immense deprivations with great steadfastness,
but when we sense that we no longer have anything to
offer to anyone, we quickly lose our grip on life. Instinc-
tively we know that the joy of life comes from the ways

in which we live together and that the pain of life comes from the many ways we fail to do that well.

It is obvious that our brokenness is often most painfully experienced with respect to our sexuality. My own and my friends' struggles make it clear how central our sexuality is to the way we think and feel about ourselves. Our sexuality reveals to us our enormous yearning for communion. The desires of our body — to be touched, embraced, and safely held — belong to the deepest longings of the heart and are very concrete signs of our search for oneness. It is precisely around this yearning for communion that we experience so much anguish. Our society is so fragmented, our family lives so sundered by physical and emotional distance, our friendships so sporadic, our intimacies so "in-between" things and often so utilitarian, that there are few places where we can feel truly safe. I notice in myself how often my body is tense, how I usually keep my guard up, and how seldom I have a complete feeling of being at home. If I then turn to the Toronto suburbs where I live and see the pretentious mega-houses, the ugly shopping malls strewn about to make consumption more efficient, and the alluring billboards promising comfort and relaxation in very seductive ways — all of that while forests are demolished, streams dried up, deer and rabbits and birds driven out of my environment — I am not surprised that my body screams for a healing touch and a reassuring embrace. When everything about us overstimulates and overextends our senses and when what is offered to us for the fulfillment of our deeper needs generally has about it a slightly seductive character, it is no wonder that we are plagued by crazy fantasies, wild dreams, and disturbing feelings and thoughts. It is where we are most needy and vulnerable that we most experience our brokenness. The fragmentation and commercialization of our milieu makes it nearly impossible to find a place where our whole being — body, mind, and heart — can feel safe and protected. Whether we walk on the streets of New York or Toronto, it is hard not to be pulled out of our center and experience in our own bellies the anguish and agony of our world.

The AIDS epidemic is probably one of the most telling symptoms of our contemporary brokenness. There love and death cling to each other in a violent embrace.

Young people, desperate to find intimacy and communion, risk their very lives for it. It seems that there is a cry reverberating through the large, empty spaces of our society: It is better to die than to live in constant loneliness.

Seeing AIDS patients die and seeing the spontaneous generosity with which their friends form community to support them with affection and material and spiritual help, I often wonder if this horrendous illness is not a clear summons to conversion directed to a world doomed by competition, rivalry and ever-increasing isolation. Yes, the AIDS crisis demands a wholly new look at our human brokenness.

How can we respond to this brokenness? I'd like to suggest two ways: first, befriending it and, second, putting it under the blessing. I hope you will be able to practice these ways in your own life. I have tried and try constantly, sometimes with more success than others, but I am convinced that these ways point in the right direction as means for dealing with our brokenness.

The first response, then, to our brokenness is to face it squarely and befriend it. This may seem quite unnatural. Our first, most spontaneous response to pain and suffering is to avoid it, to keep it at arm's length; to ignore, circumvent, or deny it. Suffering — be it physical, mental, or emotional — is almost always experienced as an unwelcome intrusion into our lives, something that should not be there. It is difficult, if not impossible, to see anything positive in suffering; it must be avoided at all costs.

When this is, indeed, our spontaneous attitude toward our brokenness, it is no surprise that befriending it seems, at first, masochistic. Still, my own pain in life has taught me that the first step to healing is not a step away from the pain, but a step toward it. When brokenness is, in fact, just as intimate a part of our being as our chosenness and our blessedness, we have to dare to overcome our fear and become familiar with it. Yes, we have to find the courage to embrace our own brokenness, to make our most feared enemy into a friend, and to claim it as an intimate companion. I am convinced that healing is often so difficult because we don't want to know the pain. Although this is true of all pain, it is especially true of the pain that comes from a broken heart. The anguish and agony that result from rejection, separation, neglect, abuse, and emotional manipulation serve only to paralyze us when we can't face them and keep running away from them. When we need guidance in our suffering, it is first of all a guidance that leads us closer to our pain and makes us aware that we do not have to avoid it, but can befriend it.

I remember vividly the day that I came to your house, and you had just come to the realization that your marriage had come to an end. Your suffering was immense. You saw a life-dream evaporate; you no longer had any

The first step to healing is not a step away from the pain, but a step toward it.

sense of a meaningful future; you felt lonely, guilty, anxious, ashamed, and deeply betrayed. The pain was etched on your face. It was the hardest moment of your life. I happened to be in New York and dropped in on you. What could I say? I knew that any suggestion that you would get over it, that there were still good things to think about, or that things weren't as bad as they seemed would be completely useless. I knew that the only thing I could do was to be with you, stay with you, and somehow encourage you not to run away from your pain, but to trust that you had the strength to stand in it. Now, many years later, you can say that, indeed, you could stand in your pain and grow strong through it. At the moment, it seemed an impossible task, and, still, it was the only task to which I could call you.

My own experience with anguish has been that facing it and living it through is the way to healing. But I cannot do that on my own. I need someone to keep me standing in it, to assure me that there is peace beyond the anguish, life beyond death, and love beyond fear. But I know now, at least, that attempting to avoid, repress, or escape the pain is like cutting off a limb that could be healed with proper attention.

The deep truth is that our human suffering need not be an obstacle to the joy and peace we so desire, but can become, instead, the means *to* it. The great secret of the spiritual life, the life of the Beloved Sons and Daughters of God, is that everything we live, be it gladness or sadness, joy or pain, health or illness, can all be part of the journey toward the full realization of our humanity. It is not hard to say to one another: "All that is good and beautiful leads us to the glory of the children of God." But it is very hard to say: "But didn't you know that we all have to suffer and thus enter into our glory?" Nonetheless, real care means the willingness to help each other in making our brokenness into the gateway to joy.

The second response to our brokenness is to put it under the blessing. For me, this "putting of our brokenness under the blessing" is a precondition for befriending it. Our brokenness is often so frightening to face because we live it under the curse. Living our brokenness under the curse means that we experience our pain as a confirmation of our negative feelings about ourselves. It is like saying, "I always suspected that I was useless or worthless, and now I am sure of it because of what is happening to me." There is always something in us searching for an explanation of what takes place in our lives and, if we have already yielded to the temptation to self-rejection, then every form of misfortune only deepens it. When we lose a family member or friend through death, when we become jobless, when we fail an examination, when we live through a separation or a divorce, when a war breaks out, an earthquake destroys our home or touches us, the question "Why?" spontaneously emerges. "Why me?" "Why now?" "Why here?" It is so arduous to live without an answer to this "Why?" that we are easily seduced into connecting the events over which we have no control with our conscious or unconscious evaluation. When we have cursed ourselves or have allowed others to curse us, it is very tempting to explain all the brokenness we experience as an expression or confirmation of this curse. Before we fully realize it, we have already said to ourselves: "You see, I always thought I was no good.... Now I know for sure. The facts of life prove it."

The great spiritual call of the Beloved Children of God is to pull their brokenness away from the shadow of the curse and put it under the light of the blessing. This is not as easy as it sounds. The powers of the darkness around us are strong, and our world finds it easier to manipulate self-rejecting people than self-accepting people. But when we keep listening attentively to the voice calling us the Beloved, it becomes possible to live our brokenness, not as a confirmation of our fear that we are worthless, but as an opportunity to purify and deepen the blessing that rests upon us. Physical, mental, or emotional pain lived under the blessing is experienced in ways radically different from physical, mental, or emotional pain lived under the curse. Even a small burden, perceived as a sign of our worthlessness, can lead us to deep depression — even suicide. However, great and heavy burdens become light and easy when they are lived in the light of the blessing. What seemed intolerable becomes a challenge. What seemed a reason for depression becomes a source of purification. What seemed punishment becomes a gentle pruning. What seemed rejection becomes a way to a deeper communion.

And so the great task becomes that of allowing the blessing to touch us in our brokenness. Then our brokenness will gradually come to be seen as an opening toward the full acceptance of ourselves as the Beloved. This explains why true joy can be experienced in the midst of great suffering. It is the joy of being disciplined, purified, and pruned. Just as athletes who experience great pain as they run the race can, at the same time, taste the joy of knowing that they are coming closer to their goal, so also can the Beloved experience suffering as a way to the deeper communion for which they yearn. Here joy and sorrow are no longer each other's opposites, but have become the two sides of the same desire to grow to the fullness of the Beloved.

The different twelve-step programs, such as Alcoholics Anonymous, Adult Children of Alcoholics, and Overeaters Anonymous, are all ways of putting our brokenness under the blessing and thereby making it a way to new life. All addictions make us slaves, but each time we confess openly our dependencies and express our trust that God can truly set us free, the source of our suffering becomes the source of our hope.

I vividly remember how I had, at one time, become totally dependent on the affection and friendship of one person. This dependency threw me into a pit of great anguish and brought me to the verge of a very self-destructive depression. But from the moment I was helped to experience my interpersonal addiction as an expression of a need for total surrender to a loving God who would fulfill the deepest desires of my heart, I started to live my dependency in a radically new way. Instead of living it in shame and embarrassment, I was able to live it as an urgent invitation to claim God's unconditional love for myself, a love I can depend on without any fear.

Well, my dear friend, I wonder if I have helped you by speaking in this way about our brokenness. Befriending it and putting it under the blessing do not necessarily make our pain less painful. In fact, it often makes us more aware of how deep the wounds are and how unrealistic it is to expect them to vanish. Living with mentally handicapped people has made me more and more aware of how our wounds are often an essential part of the fabric of our lives. The pain of parental rejection, the suffering of not being able to marry, the anguish of always needing help even in the most "normal" things such as dressing, eating, walking, taking a bus, buying a gift, or paying a bill — none of this brokenness will ever go away or become less. And still, embracing it and bringing it into the light of the One who calls us the Beloved can make our brokenness shine like a diamond.

Do you remember how, two years ago, we went to Lincoln Center and heard Leonard Bernstein conducting music by Tschaikovsky? It was a very moving evening. Later we realized that it was the last time we were to hear this musical genius. Leonard Bernstein was, no doubt, one of the most influential conductors and composers in introducing me to the beauty and the joy of music. As a teenager, I was completely taken by the enthusiastic way in which he played the role of both conductor and soloist in a performance of the Mozart piano concertos at the Kurhaus Concert Hall in Scheveningen, Holland. When his *West Side Story* appeared on the screen, I found myself humming its captivating melodies for months afterward, returning to the cinema whenever I could.

Watching his expressive face on TV while he directed and explained classical music for children, I realized how much Leonard Bernstein had become my most revered music teacher. It is no surprise, therefore, that his sudden death hit me as that of a very personal friend.

As I write you now about our brokenness, I recall a

"I never realized that broken glass could shine so brightly."

scene from Leonard Bernstein's *Mass* (a musical work written in memory of John F. Kennedy) that embodied for me the thought of brokenness put under the blessing. Toward the end of this work, the priest, richly dressed in splendid liturgical vestments, is lifted up by his people. He towers high above the adoring crowd, carrying in his hands a glass chalice. Suddenly, the human pyramid collapses, and the priest comes tumbling down. His vestments are ripped off, and his glass chalice falls to the ground and is shattered. As he walks slowly through the debris of his former glory — barefoot, wearing only blue jeans and a T-shirt — children's voices are heard singing, "Laude, laude, laude" — "Praise, praise, praise." Suddenly the priest notices the broken chalice. He looks at it for a long time and then, haltingly, he says, "I never realized that broken glass could shine so brightly."

Those words I will never forget. For me, they capture the mystery of my life, of your life, and now, shortly after his death, of Bernstein's own splendid but tragic life.

Before concluding these words about our brokenness, I want to say again something about its implications for our relationships with other people. As I grow older, I am more than ever aware of how little as well as how much we can do for others. Yes indeed, we are chosen, blessed, and broken to be given. And it is this I want to speak of now.

GIVEN

We are chosen, blessed, and broken so as to be given. The fourth aspect of the life of the Beloved is to be given. For me, personally, this means that it is only as people who are given that we can fully understand our being chosen, blessed, and broken. In the giving it becomes clear that we are chosen, blessed, and broken not simply for our own sakes, but so that all we live finds its final significance in its being lived for others.

Both of us know from experience the joy that comes from being able to do something for another person. You have done much for me, and I will always be grateful to you for what you have given me. Part of my gratitude, however, is the result of seeing you so happy in giving me so much. It is so much easier to be grateful for a gift given in joy than for a gift given with hesitation or reluctance. Have you ever noticed the joy of a mother when she sees her baby smile? The baby's smile is a gift to the mother who is grateful to see her baby so happy!

What a wonderful mystery this is! Our greatest fulfillment lies in giving ourselves to others. Although it often seems that people give only to receive, I believe that, beyond all our desires to be appreciated, rewarded, and acknowledged, there lies a simple and pure desire to give. I remember how I once spent long hours looking in Dutch stores for a birthday gift for my father or mother, simply enjoying being able to give. Our humanity comes to its fullest bloom in giving. We become beautiful people when we give whatever we can give: a smile, a handshake, a kiss, an embrace, a word of love, a present, a part of our life ... all of our life. I saw this most movingly on the day you and Robin got married. It was the day on which the grief over the failure of your first marriage came to an end and you were able to fully reclaim the truth that life finds its fulfillment in giving. The afternoon before the wedding, you picked me up from La Guardia Airport, took me to dinner with your mother, your sister, your brother-in-law, and your little niece and drove me out to the hotel to spend the night before the celebration. It was a beautiful, sunny May weekend, and, although you displayed the usual nervousness of a groom before his wedding, you were peaceful and joyful. Your heart was in the anticipation of your life with Robin. You told me that Robin had given you new confidence in yourself, had taken away your doubts about loving well and finding the perfect job, and encouraged you to trust that you would find the best way to use your

Our greatest fulfillment lies in giving ourselves to others.

gifts even when you didn't fit into the traditional slots that society had to offer — and, most importantly, that Robin loved you for who you were and not just for what you would earn or accomplish. You also told me that you were aware of how great a support you had become to Robin. You admired her great commitment as a lawyer for the poor and homeless, her great gifts for defending those who have little voice in our world, and her vitality and good humor. But you were also quite aware of how you were giving her something unique that she couldn't give to herself: a home, a place of safety and fruitfulness. Your love for her was so beautiful to see, and I felt so privileged to be invited to be such a close witness to that love.

As we lived the splendid wedding day, with its moving Jewish rituals led by your rabbi friend, Helene Ferris, the joyful garden reception and the gracious dinner, I realized more than ever how true it is that our lives find their fulfillment in giving ourselves to others. That day you gave yourself to Robin, and you made it clear that, whatever might happen — be it in your work, with your health, or on the economic or political scene — Robin would, from now on, be your first concern.

Since your marriage to Robin was your second marriage and since you had lived through the long loneliness of a divorce, you were quite humble in it all. You knew that nothing good happens automatically and that giving yourself to Robin was a decision that would have to be renewed day after day, especially on days when you experienced distance between yourselves.

I also became deeply aware of how much you need family and friends to surround you with love as you and Robin live out your promises to each other. Your invitation to be so close to you on your wedding day made me aware that you wanted me to be one of the friends who would help you to be faithful, and I experienced that as a joyful responsibility.

It is sad to see that, in our highly competitive and greedy world, we have lost touch with the joy of giving. We often live as if our happiness depended on having. But I don't know anyone who is really happy because of what he or she has. True joy, happiness, and inner peace come from the giving of ourselves to others. A happy life is a life for others. That truth, however, is usually discovered when we are confronted with our brokenness.

Reflecting a little more on the way our friendship has grown over the years, I realize that there is a mysterious link between our brokenness and our ability to give to each other. We both went through periods of extreme inner pain. And during those painful times, we often felt that our lives had come to a standstill and that we had nothing to offer; but now, years later, those periods have proven to be the times that made us able to give more instead of less. Our brokenness opened us to a deeper way of sharing our lives and offering each other hope. Just as bread needs to be broken in order to be given, so, too, do our lives. But that clearly does not mean that we should inflict pain on each other or others to make us better givers. Even though a broken glass can shine brightly, only a fool will break glass to make it shine! As mortal people, brokenness is a reality of our existence, and as we befriend it and place it under the blessing, we will discover how much we have to give — much more than we may ever have dreamed.

Isn't a meal together the most beautiful expression of our desire to be given to each other in our brokenness? The table, the food, the drinks, the words, the stories: Are they not the most intimate ways in which we not only express the desire to give our lives to each other, but also to do this in actuality? I very much like the expression "breaking bread together," because there the breaking and the giving are so clearly one. When we eat together we are vulnerable to one another. Around the table we can't wear weapons of any sort. Eating from the same bread and drinking from the same cup call us to live in unity and peace. This becomes very visible when there is a conflict. Then eating and drinking together can become a truly threatening event; then the meal can become the most dreaded moment of the day. We all know about painful silences during dinner. They contrast starkly with the intimacy of eating and drinking together, and the distance between those sitting around the table can be unbearable.

On the other hand, a really peaceful and joyful meal together belongs to the greatest moments of life.

Don't you think that our desire to eat together is an expression of our even deeper desire to be food for one another? Don't we sometimes say: "That was a very nurturing conversation. That was a refreshing time"? I think that our deepest human desire is to give ourselves to each other as a source of physical, emotional, and spiritual growth. Isn't the baby at its mother's breast one of the most moving signs of human love? Isn't "tasting" the best word to express the experience of intimacy? Don't

111

lovers in their ecstatic moments experience their love as a desire to eat and drink each other? As the Beloved ones, our greatest fulfillment lies in becoming bread for

---

The real question is not "What can we offer each other?" but "Who can we be for each other?"

---

the world. That is the most intimate expression of our deepest desire to give ourselves to each other.

How can this be done? If our deepest fulfillment comes from being given as a gift for others, how do we go about living such a vision on a day-to-day basis in a society that speaks more about having than giving? I'd like to suggest two directions: giving oneself in life and giving oneself in death.

First of all, our life itself is the greatest gift to give — something we constantly forget. When we think about our being given to each other, what comes immediately to mind are our unique talents: those abilities to do special things especially well. You and I have spoken about this quite often. "What is our unique talent?" we asked. However, when focusing on talents, we tend to forget that our real gift is not so much what we can do, but who we are. The real question is not "What can we offer each other?" but "Who can we be for each other?" No doubt, it is wonderful when we can repair something for a neighbor, give helpful advice to a friend, offer wise counsel to a colleague, bring healing to a patient, or announce good news to a parishioner, but there is a greater gift than all of this. It is the gift of our own life that shines through all we do. As I grow older, I discover more and more that the greatest gift I have to offer is my own joy of living, my own inner peace, my own silence and solitude, my own sense of well-being. When I ask myself, "Who helps me most?" I must answer, "The one who is willing to share his or her life with me."

It is worthwhile making a distinction between talents and gifts. More important than our talents are our gifts. We may have only a few talents, but we have many gifts. Our gifts are the many ways in which we express our humanity. They are part of who we are: friendship, kindness, patience, joy, peace, forgiveness, gentleness, love, hope, trust, and many others. These are the true gifts we have to offer to each other.

Somehow I have known this for a long time, especially through my personal experience of the enormous healing power of these gifts. But since my coming to live in a community with mentally handicapped people, I have rediscovered this simple truth. Few, if any, of those people have talents they can boast of. Few are able to make contributions to our society that allow them to earn money, compete on the open market, or win awards. But how splendid are their gifts! Bill, who suffered intensely as a result of shattered family relationships, has a gift for friendship that I have seldom experienced. Even when I grow impatient or distracted by other people, he remains always faithful and continues to support me in all I do. Linda, who has a speech handicap, has a unique gift for welcoming people. Many who have stayed in our community remember Linda as the one who made them feel at home. Adam, who is unable to speak, walk, or eat without help and who needs constant support, has the great gift of bringing peace to those who care for him and live with him. The longer I live in L'Arche, the more I recognize the true gifts that in us, seemingly non-handicapped people, often remain buried beneath our talents. The so-visible brokenness of our handicapped people has, in some mysterious way, allowed them to offer their gifts freely and without inhibition.

More surely than ever before, I know now that we are called to give our very lives to one another and that, in so doing, we become a true community of love.

Second, we are called to give ourselves, not only in life, but in death as well. As the Beloved Children of God, we are called to make our death the greatest gift. Since it is true that we are broken so as to be given, then our final brokenness, death, is to become the means to our final gift of self. How can that be true? It seems that death is the great enemy to be evaded for as long as possible. Dying is not something we like to think about or talk about. Still, one of the very few things we can be sure of is that we will die. I am constantly amazed by the lengths to which our society goes to prevent us from preparing ourselves well for death.

For the Beloved Sons and Daughters of God, dying is the gateway to the complete experience of being the Beloved. For those who know they are chosen, blessed, and broken to be given, dying is the way to becoming pure gift.

I do not think that you and I have spoken much about death. It seems far away, unreal — something more for others than for us. Even though the media confront us daily with the tragic reality of countless people dying through violence, war, starvation and neglect, and even though we hear regularly that people in our own circle of family and friends have died, we pay very little attention to our own approaching death. In our society we barely take the time to mourn when a friend or family member dies. Everything around us encourages us to keep going "as if nothing has happened." But then we never come in touch with our mortality, and when, finally, we have to face our own approaching death, we try to deny it as long as possible and are perplexed, yes even angry, when we cannot escape it.

Still, as the Beloved, I am called to trust that life is a preparation for death as a final act of giving. Not only are we called to live for others, but also to die for others. How is this possible?

Let me tell you first about two dear friends who have died during the past few months: Murray McDonnell and Pauline Vanier. I miss them. Their deaths are a painful loss. Whenever I think of them, I feel the biting pain that they are no longer in their homes with their families and friends. I can no longer call them, visit them, hear their voices or see their faces. I feel immense grief. But I believe deeply that their deaths are more than a loss. Their deaths are also a gift.

The deaths of those whom we love and who love us open up the possibility of a new, more radical communion, a new intimacy, a new belonging to each other. If love is, indeed, stronger than death, then death has the potential to deepen and strengthen the bonds of love. It was only after Jesus had left his disciples that they were able to grasp what he truly meant to them. But isn't that true for all who die in love?

It is only when we have died that our spirits can completely reveal themselves. Murray and Pauline were both beautiful people, but they were also people whose ability to love was limited by their many needs and wounds. Now, after their deaths, the needs and wounds that kept their spirits captive no longer inhibit them from giving their full selves to us. Now they can send us their spirits, and we can live in a new communion with them.

None of this happens without preparation. I know this because I have seen people die in anger and bitterness and with a great unwillingness to accept their mortality. Their deaths became sources of frustration and even guilt for those who stayed behind. Their deaths never became a gift. They had little to send. The spirit has been extinguished by the powers of darkness.

Yes, there is such a thing as a good death. We ourselves are responsible for the way we die. We have to choose between clinging to life in such a way that death becomes nothing but a failure, or letting go of life in freedom so that we can be given to others as a source of hope. This is a crucial choice and we have to "work" on that choice every day of our lives. Death does not have to be our final failure, our final defeat in the struggle of life, our unavoidable fate. If our deepest human desire is, indeed, to give ourselves to others, then we can make our death into a final gift. It is so wonderful to see how fruitful death is when it is a free gift.

For Murray, who died very suddenly from heart failure, the last five years of his life were a preparation for his death. He had become increasingly vulnerable to his wife, Peggy, his nine children and their families, and to all those he loved. He also had found in himself the courage to make peace with all he had struggled with. His great openness to me, his sincere interest in my life with mentally handicapped people, and his generous support of my writing had established a deep bond of friendship between us. I could hardly think of his not being there for me. Still, his death, shocking as it was, became a celebration of love. When his whole family gathered again a year after his death, everyone had beautiful stories to tell about how Murray had given much new life and new hope to all who mourned his leaving.

Pauline Vanier was ninety-three when she died. As the wife of the former governor-general of Canada, she had lived among the great and powerful of this world. But when, after the death of her husband, she joined her son Jean in his community with the weak and powerless, she became grandmother, mother, friend, and confidante of many. During the year I lived in her house, she offered me much of her care and shared with me much of her wisdom. Coming to L'Arche will always be connected for me with loving "Mammie." Although I miss her, I know

---

We are called to become bread for each other — bread for the world.

---

that the fruits of her life will become more and more evident in my life and in the lives of all who were so close to her, and I trust that her spirit, so full of humor and prayer, will continue to guide us.

The death of the Beloved bears fruit in many lives. You and I have to trust that our short little lives can bear fruit far beyond the boundaries of our chronologies. But we have to choose this and trust deeply that we have a spirit to send that will bring joy, peace, and life to those who will remember us. Francis of Assisi died in 1226, but he is still very much alive! His death was a true gift, and today, nearly eight centuries later, he continues to fill his brothers and sisters, within and outside the Franciscan orders, with great energy and life. He died, but never died. His life goes on bearing new fruit around the world. His spirit keeps descending upon us. More than ever I am convinced that death can, indeed, be chosen as our final gift of life.

You and I have only a short time left to live. The twenty, thirty, forty, or fifty years that are still ahead of us will go by very quickly. We can act as if we are to live forever and be surprised when we don't, but we can also live with the joyful anticipation that our greatest desire to live our lives for others can be fulfilled in the way we choose to die. When it is a death in which we lay down our life in freedom, we and all we love will discover how much we have to give.

We are chosen, blessed, and broken to be given, not only in life, but in death as well. As the Beloved Children of God, we are called to become bread for each other — bread for the world. This vision gives a new dimension to the Elisha story of the multiplication of the loaves.

Elisha said to the servant who came with twenty barley loaves and fresh grain still in the husk: "Give it to the company to eat." When the servant protested: "How can I serve this to a hundred men?" Elisha insisted: "Give it to the company." He served them; they ate and had some left over.

Is this story not the true story of the spiritual life? We may be little, insignificant servants in the eyes of a world motivated by efficiency, control, and success. But when we realize that God has chosen us from all eternity, sent us into the world as the blessed ones, handed us over to suffering, can't we, then, also trust that our little lives will multiply themselves and be able to fulfill the needs of countless people? This might sound pompous and self-aggrandizing, but, in truth, the trust in one's fruitfulness emerges from a humble spirit. It is the humble spirit of Hannah who exclaimed in gratitude for the new life born in her: "My spirit exults in God my savior — he has looked upon his lowly handmaid — and done great things for me ... from this day forward all generations will call me blessed." The fruitfulness of our little life, once we recognize it and live it as the life of the

122

Beloved, is beyond anything we ourselves can imagine. One of the greatest acts of faith is to believe that the few years we live on this earth are like a little seed planted in a very rich soil. For this seed to bear fruit, it must die. We often see or feel only the dying, but the harvest will be abundant even when we ourselves are not the harvesters.

How different would our life be were we truly able to trust that it multiplied in being given away! How different would our life be if we could but believe that every little act of faithfulness, every gesture of love, every word of forgiveness, every little bit of joy and peace will multiply and multiply as long as there are people to receive it ... and that — even then — there will be leftovers!

Imagine yourself as being deeply convinced that your love for Robin, your kindness to your friends, and your generosity to the poor are little mustard seeds that will become strong trees in which many birds can build their nests! Imagine that, in the center of your heart, you trust that your smiles and handshakes, your embraces and your kisses are only the early signs of a worldwide community of love and peace! Imagine that your trusting that every little movement of love you make will ripple out into ever new and wider circles — just as a little stone thrown into a still pond. Imagine, imagine.... Could you ever be depressed, angry, resentful, or vengeful? Could you ever hate, destroy, or kill? Could you ever despair of the meaning of your short earthly existence?

You and I would dance for joy were we to know truly that we, little people, are chosen, blessed, and broken to become the bread that will multiply itself in the giving. You and I would no longer fear death, but live toward it as the culmination of our desire to make all of ourselves a gift for others. The fact that we are so far from that state of mind and heart shows only that we are mere beginners in the spiritual life and have not yet fully claimed the full truth of our call. But let us be thankful for every little glimpse of the truth that we can recognize and trust that there is always more to see — always.

Within a few years, we both will be buried or cremated. The houses in which we live will probably still be there, but someone else will live there and most likely know little or nothing about us. But I believe, and I hope you will too, that our brief, easily forgotten journey in this world will continue to give life to people through all times and places. The spirit of love, once freed from our mortal bodies, will blow where it will, even when few will hear its coming and going.

Living as the Beloved

AS THOSE WHO ARE CHOSEN, blessed, broken, and given, we are called to live our lives with a deep inner joy and peace. It is the life of the Beloved, lived in a world constantly trying to convince us that the burden is on us to prove that we are worthy of being loved.

But what of the other side of it all? What of our desire to build a career, our hope for success and fame, and our dream of making a name for ourselves? Is that to be despised? Are these aspirations in opposition to the spiritual life?

Some people might answer "Yes" to that question and

counsel you to leave the fast pace of the big city and look for a milieu where you can pursue the spiritual life without restraints. But I don't think that that's your way. I don't believe that your place is in a monastery or a community such as L'Arche or the solitude of the countryside. I would say, even, that the city with its challenges is not such a bad place for you and your friends. There is stimulation, excitement, movement, and a lot to see, hear, taste, and enjoy. The world is evil only when you become its slave. The world has a lot to offer — just as Egypt did for the children of Jacob — as long as you don't feel bound to obey it. The great struggle facing you is not to leave the world, to reject your ambitions and aspirations, or to despise money, prestige, or success, but to claim your spiritual truth and to live in the world as someone who doesn't belong to it. It is exciting to win a competition, it is interesting to meet influential people, it is inspiring to listen to a concert at Lincoln Center, to see a movie, or to visit a new exhibition at the Metropolitan. And what's wrong with good friends, good food, and good clothes?

I believe deeply that all the good things our world has

to offer are yours to enjoy. But you can enjoy them truly only when you can acknowledge them as affirmations of the truth that you are the Beloved of God. That truth will set you free to receive the beauty of nature and

The world is evil only when you become its slave.

culture in gratitude, as a sign of your Belovedness. That truth will allow you to receive the gifts you receive from your society and celebrate life. But that truth will also allow you to let go of what distracts you, confuses you, and puts in jeopardy the life of the Spirit within you.

Think of yourself as having been sent into the world ... a way of seeing yourself that is possible if you truly believe that you were loved before the world began ... a perception of yourself that calls for a true leap of faith! As long as you live in the world, yielding to its enormous pressures to prove to yourself and to others that you are somebody and knowing from the beginning that you will lose in the end, your life can be scarcely more than a long struggle for survival. If, however, you really want to *live* in the world, you cannot look to the world itself as the source of that life. The world and its strategies may help you to survive for a long time, but they cannot help you live because the world is not the source even of its own life, let alone yours.

Spiritually you do not belong to the world. And this is precisely why you are sent into the world. Your family and your friends, your colleagues and your competitors, and all the people you may meet on your journey through life are all searching for more than survival. Your presence among them as the one who is sent will allow them to catch a glimpse of the real life.

Everything changes radically from the moment you know yourself as being sent into this world. Times and spaces, people and events, art and literature, history and science, they all cease to be opaque and become transparent, pointing far beyond themselves to the place from where you come and to where you will return. It is very hard for me to explain to you this radical change because it is a change that cannot be described in ordinary terms; nor can it be taught or practiced as a new discipline of self-knowledge. The change of which I speak is the change from living life as a painful test to *prove* that you deserve to be loved, to living it as an unceasing "*Yes*" to the truth of that Belovedness. Put simply, life is a God-given opportunity to become who we are, to affirm our own true spiritual nature, claim our truth, appropriate and integrate the reality of our being, but, most of all, to say "Yes" to the One who calls us the Beloved.

The unfathomable mystery of God is that God is a Lover who wants to be loved. The one who created us is waiting for our response to the love that gave us our being. God not only says: "You are my Beloved." God also asks: "Do you love me?" and offers us countless chances to say "Yes." That is the spiritual life: the chance to say "Yes" to our inner truth. The spiritual life, thus understood, radically changes everything. Being born and growing up, leaving home and finding a career, being praised and being rejected, walking and resting, praying and playing, becoming ill and being healed — yes, living and dying — they all become expressions of that divine question: "Do you love me?" And at every point of the journey there is the choice to say "Yes" and the choice to say "No."

Once you are able to catch a glimpse of this spiritual vision, you can see how the many distinctions that are so central in our daily living lose their meaning. When joy and pain are both opportunities to say "Yes" to our divine childhood, then they are more alike than they are different. When the experience of being awarded a prize and the experience of being found lacking in excellence both offer us a chance to claim our true identity as the "Beloved" of God, these experiences are more similar than they are different. When feeling lonely and feeling at home both hold a call to discover more fully who the God is whose children we are, these feelings are more united than they are distinct. When, finally, both living and dying bring us closer to the full realization of our spiritual selfhood, they are not the great opposites the world would have us believe; they are, instead, two sides of the same mystery of God's love. Living the spiritual life means living life as one unified reality. The forces of darkness are the forces that split, divide, and set in opposition. The forces of light unite. Literally, the word "diabolic" means dividing. The demon divides; the Spirit unites.

The spiritual life counteracts the countless divisions that pervade our daily life and cause destruction and violence. These divisions are interior as well as exterior: the divisions among our most intimate emotions and the divisions among the most widespread social groupings. The division between gladness and sadness within me or the division between the races, religions, and cultures around me all find their source in the diabolic forces of darkness. The Spirit of God, the Spirit that calls us the Beloved, is the Spirit that unites and makes whole. There is no clearer way to discern the presence of God's Spirit than to identify the moments of unification, healing, restoration, and reconciliation. Wherever the Spirit works, divisions vanish and inner as well as outer unity manifests itself.

What I most want to say is that when the totality of our daily lives is lived "from above," that is, as the Beloved sent into the world, then everyone we meet and everything that happens to us becomes a unique opportunity to choose for the life that cannot be conquered by death. Thus, both joy and suffering become part of the way to our spiritual fulfillment. I found this vision movingly expressed by the novelist Julien Green in a letter to his friend, the French philosopher Jacques Maritain. He writes: "When you think of the mystical experience of many saints, you may ask yourself whether joy and suffering aren't aspects of the same phenomenon on a very high level. An analogy, crazy for sure, comes to my mind: Extreme cold burns. It seems nearly certain, no, it is certain, that we can only go to God through suffering and that this suffering becomes joy because it finally is the same thing."*

Where does all this lead us? I think that it leads us back to the "place" we come from, the "place" of God. We are sent into this world for a short time to say — through the joys and pains of our clock-time — the great "Yes" to the love that has been given to us and in so doing return to the One who sent us with that "Yes" engraved on our hearts. Our death thus becomes the

---

*Une grand amitié: Correspondance 1926–1972, Julien Green–Jacques Maritain (Paris: Gallimard, 1982), 282.

moment of return. But our death can be this only if our whole life has been a journey back to the One from whom we come and who calls us the Beloved. There is such confusion about the idea of a life "hereafter," or "the eternal life." Personally, I do believe deeply in the eternal life, but not simply as a life after our physical death. It is only when we have claimed for ourselves the life of God's Spirit during the many moments of our "chronology" that we expect death to be the door to the fullness of life. Eternal life is not some great surprise that comes unannounced at the end of our existence in time; it is, rather, the full revelation of what we have been and have lived all along. The evangelist John expresses this succinctly when he says: "My dear people, what we are to be in the future has not yet been recorded; all we know is that, when it is recorded, we shall be like him because we shall see him as he really is."

With this vision, death is no longer the ultimate de-feat. To the contrary, it becomes the final "Yes" and the great return to where we can most fully become children of God. I don't think that many people look at death this way. Instead of seeing it as a moment of fulfillment, they fear it as the great failure to be kept at bay for as long as possible. All that our society has to say suggests that death is the great enemy who will finally get the better of us against our will and desire. But thus perceived, life is little more than a losing battle, a hopeless

Eternal life is the full revelation of what we have been and have lived all along.

struggle, a journey of despair. My own vision and yours too, I hope, is radically different. Even though I often give in to the many fears and warnings of my world, I still believe deeply that our few years on this earth are part of a much larger event that stretches out far beyond the boundaries of our birth and death. I think of it as a mission into time, a mission that is very exhilarating and even exciting, mostly because the One who sent me on the mission is waiting for me to come home and tell the story of what I have learned.

Am I afraid to die? I am every time I let myself be seduced by the noisy voices of my world telling me that my "little life" is all I have and advising me to cling to it with all my might. But when I let these voices move to the background of my life and listen to that small soft voice calling me the Beloved, I know that there is nothing to fear and that dying is the greatest act of love, the act that leads me into the eternal embrace of my God whose love is everlasting.

Epilogue

A Friendship Deepens

After having finished *Life of the Beloved,* I sent it to Fred, anxiously wondering whether I had been able to respond to his request: "Say something about the Spirit that my secular friends and I can hear." I had tried to speak from my heart to his heart, from my own most personal experience to his, from my true self to his true self. I was very curious to know whether I had succeeded.

Shortly after Fred had received the text, he called me and offered to come to Toronto to spend a few days in the community and talk about "the life of the Beloved." When he came, we became aware that the past decade had brought us to a place much more solid than when we first met. I had found a true home in L'Arche, and Fred was happily married, waiting for his first child and satisfied in his job. He had published two books for teenagers, one about the Gulf War and another about losing a parent, and he was preparing a book in which leaders and experts in fields as different as politics, the arts, literature, and sports recommend the best books to read. He was even using his early morning hours to work on a novel! His dream of becoming a writer has, in fact, come true, though in a way different from what he had anticipated.

Both of us had grown a lot. We had become less insecure and more rooted. But we also had become more aware of the distance between us. During our long conversations about the text of this book, it became increasingly clear that, although Fred had many good things to say about my words to him, I had not been able to do what he had hoped for. He had shown the manuscript to two of his friends, and it was clear that neither of them had been deeply touched. As we talked more, Fred convinced me that this book was not as radically different from my previous books as I had assumed. Fred had always liked my writing, but never as writing that spoke directly to his own needs. For him, it was writing for the "converted" and not for truly secular people. He felt this book wasn't very different in this respect.

I was very disappointed that the gap between us, when it concerned the spiritual life, was so much greater than I had thought. I had so much hoped that, after our long years as friends, I would have been able to find the words to bridge that gap. I had so much hoped that I would have been able to speak to Fred and his friends in a way that would open in them a true desire to develop a life in the Spirit.

Why had I not been able to speak to the most basic concerns of Fred and his friends? Fred was very gentle about it, very aware of my sensitivities, but also very clear. He said, "Although it is clear that you try to write for me and my friends from your own center and although you express to us what is most precious to you, you do not realize how far we are from where you are. You speak from a context and tradition that is alien to us, and your words are based on many presuppositions that we don't share with you. You are not aware of how truly secular we are. Many, many questions need to be answered before we are able to be fully open to what you say about the life of the Beloved."

It wasn't easy to hear this criticism, but I wanted to

listen to it in a nondefensive way so that I could discover in my own heart where I was being challenged. My attempt had been to be a "witness of God's love" to a secular world, but I had sounded like someone who is so excited about the art of sailing that he forgets that his listeners have never seen lakes or the sea, not to mention sailboats!

Fred tried to explain the problem. "Long before you start speaking about being the Beloved and becoming the

The issue is whether there is anything in our world that we can call "sacred."

Beloved, you have to respond to some very fundamental questions such as: Who is God? Who am I? Why am I here? How can I give my life meaning? How do I get faith? When you do not help us to answer these questions, your beautiful meditations on being and becoming the Beloved remain dreamlike for us."

Fred said many other things, but the main response to all I had written was that I had not truly entered into the secular mentality. When I am honest with my experiences among my nephews and nieces in Holland, my business friends in Canada and the United States, and my many correspondents from all over the world, I have to confess that Fred's criticism would most likely be affirmed by many of them. The issue is no longer how to express the mystery of God to people who are no longer accustomed to the traditional language of church or synagogue; the issue is whether there is anything in our world that we can call "sacred." Is there, among the things we do, the people we know, the events we read about in the newspapers or watch on TV, someone or something that transcends it all and has the inner quality of sacredness, of being holy, worthy of adoration and worship?

Fred was quite willing to say that, with the disappearance of the sacred from our world, the human imagination had been impoverished and that many people live with a sense of loss, even emptiness. But where and how can we rediscover the sacred and give it the central place in our lives? I am quite aware now that, in this book, I have not adequately responded to this question.

Could I have done so? Should I have done so? Fred and I spent a few days together in the Daybreak community. As we visited the different homes where mentally handicapped people and their assistants share their lives together, I became increasingly aware that I can speak and write only about ideas and visions that are anchored in my own daily experiences. And these experiences are completely pervaded with the knowledge of God's presence. Would I be able to step out of that God-centered reality and respond to those who say: "Do I really need God to live, to be happy, to enjoy life, to fulfill my deepest desires? Do I need faith to live a decent and creative life?"

I feel within myself a deep-rooted resistance to proving anything to anybody. I don't want to say: "I will show you that you need God to live a full life." I can only say: "For me, God is the one who calls me the Beloved, and I have a desire to express to others how I try to become more fully who I already am." But beyond that I feel very poor and powerless.

However, all of this does not mean that Fred's response to this book doesn't hold a tremendous challenge for me. It is the challenge to explore my own inner solidarity with the secular world. Although I live in a Christian community and feel quite responsible for protecting and nurturing the sacred in our common life, I am surrounded, within as well as outside the boundaries of our community, by the secular world. But more than that, I know that as much as I focus in my life on the sacred, I am also a very secular person. The questions that Fred raises are not alien to me. In fact, the more I enter into an intimate dialogue with the secular world, the more I discover my own secularity and the more I can see that Fred and his friends are not as far away from me as I might have thought.

Maybe the great challenge is to trust so much in God's love that I don't have to be afraid to enter fully into the secular world and speak there about faith, hope, and love. Maybe the place where the gap has to be bridged is within me. Maybe the distinction between secular and sacred can be bridged when they have both been identified as aspects of every person's experience of being human. Maybe I don't have to become an apologist for God's existence and the religious meaning of life in order to respond to Fred's criticism. At this moment I can say no more than that.

After Fred's visit to Daybreak, I was left with the question: What to do with this book? Forget about it, rewrite it, publish it as it is? For a long time I was quite confused.

Then something unexpected happened. Having sent it to Gordon Cosby and Diana Chambers of the Servant Leadership School of the Church of the Saviour in Washington, D.C., I received a very encouraging reply. They wrote me that this text had helped them more than previous ones and had inspired them to offer a new course in "The Life of the Beloved." Also, Bart Gavigan of the South Park Community in England responded very enthusiastically to the text. Gordon, Diana, and Bart all urged me not to change much, but just to trust that what is there will bear fruit. "What about Fred?" I asked. "Well," they answered, "you might not have been able to write all that Fred needs to hear, but Fred certainly enabled you to write what we need to hear! Couldn't you just be happy with that?"

Here the real irony of writing hit me. I had tried so hard to write something for secular people, and the ones who were most helped by it were searching Christians in Washington and London. I suddenly realized that without Fred I would never have found the words that were so helpful to believers. For me, there is more than an irony here. It is the mystery of God using his secular friends to instruct his disciples.

It was this realization that finally made me decide not to write a new book, but to trust that what is here should be published and that what is not here may one day find an authentic form of expression.

Guide for Reflection

These reflections, prepared by Crossroad, may be used for personal meditation or in small groups.

I. A Friendship Begins

a. "Suddenly it hit me that Fred was close to surrendering his dreams. He looked to me like a prisoner locked behind the bars of a society forcing him to work at something in which he didn't believe" (p. 13). Who have you known who felt trapped in their job or career? Think about the times in your life when you felt the way Fred did.

b. "You have nothing to lose. You are young, full of energy, well trained.... Everything is possible for you" (p. 15). Imagine that Nouwen is saying these words to you today. What parts of this statement connect with you in your present life?

151

II. *Being the Beloved*

a. "These negative voices are so loud and so persistent that it is easy to believe them.... It is the trap of self-rejection" (p. 31). What negative voices do you struggle with? Name some of them. In what ways do you sometimes find yourself agreeing with them?

b. "You can choose to reach out now to true inner freedom" (p. 38). Reflect on these words for the next few days. Imagine yourself reaching out to new freedom. What, practically, does this mean for you? What emotions and feelings do you experience?

III. *Becoming the Beloved*

Having seen the list of everyday tasks that Fred and Robin had to deal with in their lives (p. 46), think a bit about your own list of daily tasks and your approach to them. What would need to change so that your tasks could be transformed by "the movements of the Spirit of love"?

IV. *Taken*

a. "We have to dare to reclaim the truth that we are God's chosen ones, even when our world does not choose us" (p. 57). What makes you resist such a deep and life-giving truth?

b. "You have to keep unmasking the world around you for what it is: manipulative, controlling, power-hungry, and, in the long run, destructive" (p. 59). How does Nouwen harmonize this view of the "world" with his belief that everyday life can be seen in the light of love? What does this say to you about God's love? How do your bring God's love to the struggles of our daily life?

V. *Blessed*

"Isn't it easier for us to believe that we are cursed than that we are blessed?" (pp. 74–75). Consider the list of social ills Nouwen mentions on p. 74. Do some of these currently affect your daily life? What helps you remember your blessedness in the midst of such suffering?

VI. Broken

a. "From the moment we met, we spoke about our brokenness" (p. 85). Recall the last few conversations you've had. How much were they dominated by private and professional brokenness, and how much by joy? With whom are you safe enough to speak of your brokenness?

b. Think of one kind of brokenness in your life that you have avoided rather than "befriended" (p. 92). What stands between you and the acceptance of your brokenness? Can your prayer help you find the courage to be vulnerable to your pain?

c. "True joy can be experienced in the midst of great suffering" (pp. 98–99). Explain in your own words how joy and sorrow can "become the two sides of the same desire to grow to the fullness of the Beloved." What does this tell us about the God who can accept and love us even amid our suffering?

VII. Given

a. "True joy, happiness, and inner peace come from the giving of ourselves to others" (p. 109). Recall a time when you gave of yourself to others. How did you feel afterward about the other person and your relationship? How did you feel about yourself? Did this in any way open you more fully to God?

b. "It is only when we have died that our spirits can completely reveal themselves" (p. 117). Think of the lives of famous saints, writers, relatives, friends, or others who have inspired you. How do their lives and deaths show the truth of Nouwen's words that "the death of the Beloved bears fruit in many lives"?

VIII. Living as the Beloved

"When the totality of our daily lives is lived 'from above,' . . . then everyone we meet and everything that happens to us becomes a unique opportunity to choose for the life that cannot be conquered by death" (pp. 135–36). Have you ever met some-one who lived life "from above"? How did the presence of that person make you feel? In what ways could you live more fully in that way?

IX. A Friendship Deepens

In what ways have Nouwen's words spoken to your own spiritual life, struggles, and aspirations in a secular world? After reading this book, how would you answer Nouwen's question on p. 146: "Where and how can we rediscover the sacred and give it the central place in our lives?"

THE HENRI NOUWEN SOCIETY

Website: *www.henrinouwen.org/*
E-mail: *nouwensociety@nouwen.net*

Canadian Office:
Henri Nouwen Society
10265 Yonge Street
Richmond Hill, Ontario L4C 4Y7

USA Office:
Henri Nouwen Society
P.O. Box 230523, Ansonia Station
New York, NY 10023

ALSO BY HENRI J. M. NOUWEN

SABBATICAL JOURNEY
The Diary of His Final Year

In September 1995 Henri Nouwen embarked on a spiritual adventure. He took a year's sabbatical from Daybreak, the community for the mentally and physically handicapped where he lived and served, to write, pray, and visit family and friends. Little did he know that his odyssey would find his friends multiplying, family drawing closer, and other opportunities to express kindness so present that he had little time to write at all.

Sabbatical Journey records the flowering of friendship and prayer during Henri's final year. Wherever he goes, he is aware of goodness, even amid difficult experiences such as the loss of his beloved friend Adam. He receives kindnesses, recognizes them, is grateful for them, and returns them. To read his journal is to become his companion for a year.

"This is vintage Nouwen, filled with the vulnerable, anxious, caring outpourings of a man who treasured his priesthood and his friends above all else. His journal entries reveal his constant struggles between the pull of a desire for more solitude and prayer and his attraction to preaching and pastoral work."

— Dolores Dowling, O.S.B., *Spirit & Life*

0-8245-1878-0; $15.95 paperback, 240 pages

Please support your local bookstore, or call 1-800-707-0670.
For a free catalog, please write us at

THE CROSSROAD PUBLISHING COMPANY
481 EIGHTH AVENUE, SUITE 1550, NEW YORK, NY 10001
e-mail: promo@crossroadpublishing.com

crossroad